PAUL BUTLER
Reaching Children

SCRIPTURE UNION
130 CITY ROAD, LONDON EC1V 2NJ

© Paul Butler 1992

First published 1992

Reprinted 1994

ISBN 0 86201 815 3

All rights reserved. No part of this publication may be
reproduced, stored in a retrieval system, or transmitted, in any
form, or by any means, electronic, mechanical, photocopying,
recording or otherwise, without the prior permission of
Scripture Union.

The right of Paul Butler to be identified as author of this work
has been asserted by him in accordance with the Copyright,
Designs and Patents Act 1988.

British Library Cataloguing-in-Publication Data
A catalogue record for this book is available from the British
Library.

All Bible quotations, except where otherwise stated, are from
the Holy Bible, New International Version. Copyright © 1973,
1978, 1984 International Bible Society. Published by Hodder
and Stoughton.

Cover design and artwork by Mark Carpenter Design
Consultants.
Phototypeset by Intype, London.
Printed and bound in Great Britain by Cox & Wyman Ltd,
Reading, Berkshire.

CONTENTS

| FOREWORD |

I am one of a rare breed, I suspect, in that I always read the foreword to books. So welcome to this foreword, fellow reader. I hope that you enjoy all that follows in this book. But above all I hope and pray that something of my own passion for making Jesus known to children and their families comes through these pages.

In various ways I have now been involved in children's evangelism for twenty years. I have been a Christian for twenty-two years, having come to Christian faith just before my fifteenth birthday. So it seems that evangelism has been part of my own personal calling from the outset of my walk with Jesus. I cringe when I think of some of the mistakes I have made and ways in which I have worked at times. I am glad that God in his grace works through and, often it seems, in spite of, our human frailty. I am constantly astounded that God should use me; but somehow it seems he does.

One thing is clear in my own mind as I have written this book. God has taught and developed me over these past twenty two years and he has not finished with me yet. Even as I have written, my own thinking has further developed; by the time the book reaches you I trust I will have developed still further. In this task of making Jesus known none of us has arrived; we all must keep growing and developing. If we do not we are failing our Lord. I simply hope that the contents of the book help you in your own growth and development.

I have often mused on all the seemingly obligatory thanks yous with which forewords seem to conclude; I now understand. So many thanks go especially to Dai Lewis, who took me under his wing when I was a mere youth of seventeen; his counsel, example, encouragement and above all friendship have meant, and continue to mean, more than words can say. Thank you to all my colleagues in Scripture Union, especially in the Missions department, for their fellowship and encouragement. In particular I want to single out Tony Berry, Michael Wells and Janet Morgan for the way they have stimulated my thinking; they have in many ways contributed greatly to this book. An enormous thank you to Cathie Smith and Joan King without whose perceptive and judicious comments this book would be much the poorer, and to Campbell Grant who has gently nursed me through the labour of bringing this book finally to birth.

As ever the biggest thanks are reserved for my family: for putting up with Daddy in front of the Amstrad 9512 for hours and days on end. Caroline, David and Andrew – you are wonderful. And Rosemary – where would I be without you?

Now, fellow reader and learner, turn the page and to the real business of this book. There are children and families hungry for Jesus; I pray this book may help you, along with others, to reach them.

CHILDREN IN NEED

The phone rang. As soon as I picked it up I recognised the voice. 'Listen to this, bro',' he said excitedly, and proceeded to read a letter that he had just opened. ' "Dear. . . . , You probably won't remember me, but when I was nine, ten and eleven I came on your camps. I am writing to you now to tell you that I have just publicly professed my faith in Christ at a Confirmation service. I am now nineteen. I want to write to you to tell you because it was at camp that I first really heard about Jesus. Over the three years that I came I learned more about him and began to follow him. I had a few years afterwards when I slipped away but now I am clear that I want to follow him for the rest of my life. It was the patient, caring, unpressured way that you and others told me about Jesus that has led me to this. I cannot tell you how grateful I am." Isn't that terrific?' inquired the much-loved voice. 'It certainly is,' was my rather tame reply, as I didn't know quite how to express the excitement that was actually going on in my heart and mind as I had listened. None of the edge of that excitement has since worn off. I had been one of the leaders on the camps to which the writer referred.

The excitement comes for several reasons.

1   Every time I hear the story of someone realising God's love for them and responding to it I am thrilled.
2   Here is a story which demonstrates the real value of sharing with children the story of God's love shown to us in Jesus. The value is not in immediate response but in long-term discipleship.
3   Here, potentially, is someone who will now in their turn want to

help other children hear of Jesus, but want to do it in a way which treats children seriously as fellow human persons.

4 This particular child had come from a non-church family. She really had not known much of the Good News of Jesus when she first came to camp. It is seeing and hearing of children from such backgrounds coming to know Jesus for themselves which most excites me.

This book is unashamedly about sharing the Good News of Jesus with children. I believe that it is right and proper that children hear of Jesus and are allowed to respond to him. But it is equally a book wanting to ask some hard questions about just how such work with children should be undertaken and how children might respond.

It has been my intention, therefore, to face up to some of the hard questions which are rightly asked about children and evangelism. 'Should we evangelise children at all?' 'How do we avoid manipulation?' It has also been my intention to offer practical help as to how we may actually go about the task of sharing Jesus with children in the 1990s. But before we begin facing up to these questions let's remind ourselves of the situation that confronts us. The 1991 report commissioned by the Church of England General Synod entitled *All God's Children?* opens with these sobering words, 'Only 14% of children under 15 years of age are in a church-related activity on a typical Sunday. That is one of the findings of the 1989 English Church Census.' Even if we view this in the most positive light and assume that through such church contact children are really hearing the Good News both through the lives of the leaders/organisers and through specific learning activities, then 86% of the children in Britain are clearly *not* hearing it or seeing it lived out. It is primarily a concern for this 86% that is the driving motivation behind this book.

Even those who want to present a more positive picture by adding in all the children in church or public schools with a strong Christian emphasis need to face the fact that the church is totally out of touch with the majority of children in Britain today. Most children are rightly referred to therefore as 'unchurched' or non-church.

I believe that it is impossible to always draw a sharp distinction between the 'churched' and the 'unchurched'. There are many 'churched' children who have never really heard the gospel in a way that they can understand; and equally there are are least some 'unchurched' children who have a much clearer idea of it than we sometimes suggest. But most children and adults can rightly be described now as 'unchurched' or, as I tend to prefer, 'non-church'.

Around the world the figures can change quite markedly, but the truth is that millions of children die every year in infancy or early childhood having never heard the name of Jesus. In every country there are large numbers of children who know almost nothing about the story of Jesus. Often these children will know a great deal about other matters in life; one thinks of the children carrying and using guns in many war-torn zones, or 'playing terrorists' in Northern Ireland; the children living on rubbish dumps in the Philippines or in the sewers of Columbia; the estimated 8,000,000 children living on the streets of Brazil, some in fear of their lives; the children involved in prostitution on the streets of many apparently prosperous cities; or the computer-crazed children of the USA and the UK. They are very worldly-wise, but still children in their bodies, minds and emotions. How are we going to seek to help them hear the Good News of Jesus? Indeed what *is* the Good News for children such as these?

To help pursue answers to such questions each chapter ends with some suggested ideas to help the reader think through its contents. These could be done individually but would be more profitably done as a group. I have also offered a wide selection of further reading because the nature of this book means that the suggestions made are not pursued in great detail; the further reading is designed to offer that greater detail. Finally, by way of introduction, if this book does not lead to action it will have failed in its purpose. My longing is that we see a renewed enthusiasm for sharing Jesus with children and their families, and that such renewed enthusiasm expresses itself in many, varied, thoughtful ways so that large numbers discover for themselves just how great is God's love for them.

| **ACTIVITY** |

Take time to pray for children you know, the children of your own country and the children of the world.

| **FURTHER READING** |

All God's Children?, General Synod Board of Education and Board of Mission, National Society / Church House Publishing, 1991
Children Under Pressure, Pat Wynnejones, Triangle, 1987

Understanding Children, Maggie Durran, Marshalls, 1987
The State of the World's Children, Unicef, 1991

THE BIBLE: A CHILDREN'S CHARTER?

'Some people brought children to Jesus for him to place his hands on them, but the disciples scolded the people. When Jesus noticed this, he was angry and said to his disciples, "Let the children come to me, and do not stop them, because the Kingdom of God belongs to such as these. I assure you that whoever does not receive the Kingdom of God like a child will never enter it." Then he took the children in his arms, placed his hands on each of them, and blessed them' (Mark 10:13–16 GNB).

This is one of the most oft quoted passages from the scriptures when any group of Christians begin to talk and think about what the Bible has to say about children. But how often do we really seek to take an overall look at the Bible's teaching about children? You may surprise yourself, or perhaps horrify yourself, if you stop and think about this question: 'What does the Bible, as a whole, say about children and their relationship with God?' Why not take time, before reading further, to do that now?

Reference is made in the next sections to a wide number of passages of scripture. The range is intended to offer the reader plenty of scope for their own further study and exploration, and to avoid a simple 'proof texting' approach to the scriptures.

IN THE BEGINNING

Children and the experiences of childhood were always intended to be part of God's purpose for humankind. That may sound too obvious for comment, but to hear some people talk about children you would think they were a product of human rebellion against the Creator rather than an integral part of God's good plans for his world. This is more important than is often noted. It has always been God's plan that human beings go through the process of foetal growth, birth, babyhood, infancy and childhood. The way we grow up and develop is part of God's creative activity. We are born into the world not as instantly mature adults but as people who need care and nurture. From the outset we are dependent people; dependent on God for our very life, and dependent on fellow humans to help us grow and develop to our full potential. This dependence lasts from the cradle to the grave, but is most clearly seen in our earliest years.

Not only are children part of God's creative purposes, they are also regarded in the early chapters of Genesis as fully human. In Genesis 1:26ff we read that human beings are made 'in the image of God'. Much has been written on this phrase, but for our purposes the important point is clear. The image of God is in every human person. It is equally seen in male and female. There is an equality of all people built into creation. I personally find the argument that the image of God is only fully reflected in male and female *together* very convincing, but even if that view is not accurate the fact remains that no distinction is made between male and female so far as the image of God is concerned.

This image of God is passed on from one generation to another. Genesis 5:1–3 reminds us again that God made male and female in his likeness and then goes on to make it clear that Seth is in Adam's likeness and image. Some have seen here a contrast between the original image and likeness of God in Adam before his rebellion and the likeness now being to rebellious Adam rather than to God. This does not seem to make real sense of the text. Surely the re-emphasis on the likeness of God in verse 1 is to make it clear that anyone born in Adam's likeness must bear the likeness of God as well. In spite of the rebellion and being cast out of Eden the image of God is not lost. This certainly seems to be the implication again in Genesis 9:6. Such a high value on each human person is then echoed through the pages of scripture. Humankind may well be in rebellion against its Maker but it remains the crowning of God's creation (cf Psalm 8:5; 82:6, James 3:9).

With this immense dignity placed on every human being we need to ensure that we treat children with great respect for they bear the image of God just as much as any adult. In our work we should place equal value on every child. This will certainly have implications for the way in which we work with girls and boys; the intelligent and the less intelligent; the physically able and the physically disabled; children from all ethnic backgrounds, and so on and so on. We should work equally with all and seek to express that equality of value in every aspect of our work.

There is a further important aspect to humankind's creation in the image of God which is often forgotten. It is not simply a reflection of the value of every individual. God is revealed in this account as God-in-community; 'let *us* make man in *our* image, in *our* likeness' (Genesis 1:26). Although this understanding of God in community only finds its full expression in the New Testament with God revealed as Father, Son and Holy Spirit it is clearly hinted at here. This being the case it suggests strongly that part of being made in God's image is to be made to exist in community. This is made clearer by what follows in the creation account. Humankind is expected to expand into a whole community (Genesis 1:28), and Adam finds himself ill at ease in the Garden of Eden without a suitable companion with whom to share it (Genesis 2:20ff). Community or family life is built into the very fabric of human existence. From the outset it was intended that children should grow up within the context of a human family and community. The notion of the totally isolated human individual is not part of God's plans for the world. Human beings are social beings because God is a social God. If we fail to keep this in mind in our work with children we shall be missing a crucial part of God's way of working.

In practice this must mean that we work with children in their social, community and family context. We should work with their whole families, not simply the children on their own. In particular we must take great pains to work with the parents of young children, as this is the context in which their values and ideas will be formed, especially in the first five or so years of life. Our concern to share the Good News of Jesus with the children must be a concern to help parents live in ways which communicate something of God's loving rule within the home; to fail to do this would be to fail both children and adults alike.

But if the accounts of human beginnings tell us much of importance about the value and dignity of being human, however young, they also tell us about the darker side of being human. There are two important points to be made here.

1 Cain, Abel, Seth and all the others are born into a situation which they did not choose but which has major effects on them. The curse is already on Adam and Eve before any of the children are born. Already Adam is learning that the ground is no longer friendly and Eve soon discovers the discomforts of childbirth. Human rebellion (sin) affects the lives of the next generation whether they like it or not. Some of the harshness of life for these early people is not a consequence of their own actions or sin but because they are caught up in the complexities of humankind's sin. The same is then true down through history. For example, the suffering of the Hebrew children in Egypt due to the harsh treatment of the Pharaoh or the suffering of the Egyptian children due to God's sending of the various plagues is not a consequence of their own sin but because they become caught up in the overall impact of the human condition. It simply becomes a fact of human life that some children will suffer because of the sin of others; whether those others be specific individuals or humankind in general. This is a common thread in the prophets' messages to Israel in later years as well. Children may be in the situation they are in and may even behave the way they do because of their sinned againstness rather than because of their own sin.

2 Nevertheless these early chapters of Genesis do also suggest that children themselves choose to act in ways which contradict the image of God. Since this is reported as God's own thoughts we must take them with great seriousness; Genesis 8:21 says, 'The LORD said in his heart: "Never again will I curse the ground because of man, even though every inclination of his heart is evil from childhood." ' The implication is clear. Children *do* sin of their own accord. But God's grace reaches out to all such sinners. Grace is ever present in these opening chapters of the Bible.

So from these records of our beginnings we gain a great deal of insight into the value of all children, their social context and of how they are completely caught up in the human situation.

From these beginnings the rest of the scriptures give us further guidance on the place of children in God's purposes.

LAW, WISDOM, HISTORY AND ALL THAT

As the story of God's gracious dealings with humankind unfolds through the pages of the Old Testament we find children appearing again and again. Rarely do we find them at the centre of the stage, but reminders of their presence are never far away either. Some things emerge as apparently of central importance in considering any work with children.

1 CHILDREN BELONG

The emphasis on the individual over against the community is a modern one arising from the development of thought in the Western world. In the Old Testament, and indeed in the New as well, there is a strong awareness of membership of the wider community. Hence in Israel all males are circumcised as the sign of membership of the community of God's people from the very outset of their lives (Genesis 17). Although females are not given any physically distinguishing mark of covenant, God's promises are to them as well; the covenant with Abraham was with all his seed not just the male descendants (Genesis 12:1ff and 15:5).

Everyone is seen as part of their community at a variety of levels.

1   Everyone is the member of a family; which is in itself a community comprised of blood relatives, husbands and wives who covenant to relate together, and apparently servants / slaves who 'belonged' to that family.
2   Each family then belonged to a larger grouping – the clan.
3   Then several clans made up a tribe and the tribes together constituted the whole of Israel.

The importance attached to this ordered community is obvious when we look at the genealogies and lists of names and tribes in passages such as 1 Chronicles 1–9 or Nehemiah 7, or when we notice how people like Gideon describes themselves; 'My clan is the weakest in [the tribe of] Manasseh, and I am the least [important member] in my family' (Judges 6:15). Other examples include Saul (1 Samuel

10:17ff) and Jeremiah (1:1). The importance of this membership of the community is clear. People gained their identity from knowing to which people they belonged. They are individuals within their community rather than apart from it or over against it. There is an immense thread of solidarity within the people of God running through both Old and New Testaments. Children are part of that community. They belong.

2 CHILDREN ARE VULNERABLE

From the outset children were regarded as belonging to God's people within the covenant made by the Lord with Abraham and confirmed to Isaac and Jacob, and they were therefore seen as belonging to God himself. Children are also depicted as fully human, bearing God's image yet caught up in all of human sinfulness. We need to notice alongside this the threads of scripture which note the weakness and vulnerability of children, because of which they are to be treated differently from adults at times.

The natural weakness and vulnerability through the process of birth and infancy is clear. Infant mortality was a constant reality in the ancient world, just as it still is to the vast bulk of the world today. So it is hardly surprising that the survival of a child to the age of two or three when they were weaned was in itself a cause for rejoicing (Genesis 21:8). But the sadness of death in infancy was seen as not part of God's ideal; the vision of the future Isaiah offers includes an end to this (Isaiah 65:20).

Acknowledgement was also given to the fact that infants do not know right from wrong (Deuteronomy 1:39, Isaiah 7:14ff). They need to gain and develop a certain amount of knowledge before they can distinguish right from wrong; before they are able to make their own moral decisions. This clearly had implications for a child's responsibility. The children who leave Egypt are not held culpable for the later rebellion in the desert; indeed this exemption from responsibility applies to everyone up to twenty years old (Numbers 14:26ff). The age of twenty seems to have been of particular significance: only the men of twenty or over fought in Israel's army (Numbers 1:3; 26:2, 2 Chronicles 25:5). What we appear to have in these passages is some sense of growing accountability accorded to children. In their earliest years the accountability falls on their parents

rather than themselves, but as they grow and develop they are able
to take an increasing level of responsibility for their own behaviour
until they become totally answerable for their own actions. This
development is marked at various ages by acknowledging that a new
stage of development has been reached (eg weaning at two or three,
the changing redemption value at five [Leviticus 27:5] and twenty
and the later development of the Bar Mitzvah at twelve or thirteen.)
Alongside this limited yet growing responsibility of children there is
an acknowledgement that they are not innocent or perfect. We earlier
noted Genesis 8 but can add the references to individuals confessing
the sins of their youth (Job 13:26, Psalm 25:7). The question of
responsibility is something of a minefield, and we shall have to return
to it later. What we must note for now is that children were often
caught up in the actions of the adults and bore the consequences
when those actions brought about suffering and sadness. The
children themselves, however, were not held directly responsible.

The vulnerability and weakness is seen at its most stark in the
situation of those described as the fatherless. Alongside the widows
and aliens they are often referred to as the poor and needy. Their
weakness came, presumably, because they had lost the parents who
would provide them with their food, shelter and so on. God sides
with them and calls his people to offer them care and protection
because of their weak position. They become the responsibility of
the wider community to which they belong (Exodus 22:21-24,
Deuteronomy 10:18, Isaiah 1:17, Hosea 14:3, Amos 8:4). So all
children are seen as in some way in need of the care of their parents
and the community. They do not stand alone.

3 CARE OF CHILDREN

The care of children, as depicted in the scriptures, is primarily the
responsibility of the parents and household to which they belong. In
love for the child and in grateful response to God for this gift, care
will be taken to feed, wean, clothe, and generally provide for every
child. As children grow up so they will take part in the life of the
family household. They will play but also join in the work in the
fields, the cooking and so forth. The prophets at times make use of
this motherly and fatherly care as an image of God's relationship to
the people (Isaiah 49:15; 66:13, Hosea 11:1-3) and the histories give

us examples of parental care (eg Hannah [1 Samuel 1] and the Shunnamite woman [2 Kings 4]). Perhaps, however, the importance of the imperative to care for children is shown up best by the references to the fatherless / orphans to which we referred above.

Whilst it is clear that it was very important to simply provide the basics of life for each child, care did not stop here. It also included teaching and discipline so that the child would be equipped for the whole of life. (Much of Proverbs is addressed by a father to his son.) The vision for all children should be one in which none die young; all are decently housed and fed, and life is full of enjoyment and security (Isaiah 11:1–9; 65:17–25, Zechariah 8:1–5). At the centre of this vision is a renewed community at peace with God. In short, God's desire is for the total well-being of everyone – for *shalom*.

4 TEACHING AND DISCIPLINE OF CHILDREN

The key teachers in the life of a child were the parents and other adults within the family unit. For most of the Old Testament period there was no formal education in any modern sense. With the exile to Babylon and the development of synagogues some formal education did begin; at least for boys. But even when this occurs it seems that the household remained the base unit for teaching. Deuteronomy 6 and 11 show that a large measure of responsibility for teaching the faith is placed on the heads of the household. In a different context Proverbs also clearly makes a great deal of the authority and teaching example of the parents. It is to be noted here that both father and mother are referred to as having wisdom and authority (eg Proverbs 1:8; 6:20 and 31:10ff).

Throughout the history of the Old Testament we find references to the influence of parents over their children, even when the children are adults and in positions of authority. This must arise partly from the deep sense of respect for elders that clearly existed in Israel, but also from the impact of the influence throughout their earlier years. It shows the outworking of the fifth commandment which is given to all of Israel, not simply the children (Exodus 20:12)!

The content of the teaching appears to have been primarily that of telling and living the faith story of God's dealings with his people. It is significant that at Passover the key teaching point is to simply re-enact and retell the story through the corporate actions and words.

When one thinks of the stone memorials built from time to time in the history of Israel, the purpose was to act as a visual reminder of God's acts and the command was to retell the story (Joshua 4). We find this emphasis recalled again in the Psalms, notably Psalm 78:1ff. Telling the stories of God's wonders was crucial. Alongside this there went the teaching of the Law. But the two are closely linked. In Deuteronomy 6 the retelling of the story of the Exodus is to give the context for the Law. 'We live this way in response to the God who did this for us.' Law then is a response to God's grace, not an arbitrary set of regulations.

The prophets also recall the stories of God's saving acts to remind the people of their own day of what God is like and what he expects of them in response. At times they do not simply tell the message, they also act it out (eg Jeremiah 13 and 18, Hosea 1 and 3, Amos 8). Clearly they were preaching primarily to the adults but the similarity of pattern is worth noting.

The Wisdom literature teaches many of life's lessons with wisdom based on the experience and tradition of the people as they have sought to live out God's ways down through the ages.

Teaching apparently happened both formally, as in Nehemiah 8 and at Passover, or more informally as part of everyday life (Deuteronomy 6:7). The Jews were also more than happy to use visual aids to remind them of their stories and laws (Deuteronomy 6:8f) and the prophets used them to make their message clear (Jeremiah 18).

One aspect of teaching was that of **discipline**. It is clear that this was regarded as very important in the upbringing of children. This discipline was properly given in the context of loving relationships as a reflection of God's loving discipline of his children (Deuteronomy 8:5, Proverbs 3:11f). Its purpose was the well-being of God's people. It was to correct them when they wandered from God's ways, so that they might return to those ways. God's discipline took the form of reminders, rebukes, and warnings. Only when the people wilfully and persistently ignored him did he inflict punishment on them. The implication is that parental discipline of children should also have at its heart a concern for the child's well-being. It too would consist of teaching, reminders, rebukes and warnings and, at times, punishment. Just as God's punishment could take various forms (eg the withholding of a blessing like rain or crops, or – ultimately – defeat in battle) so too parental punishment could have taken a variety of forms. The famed use of the rod in Proverbs 13:24 and 22:15 is not the sole word on means of punishment as discipline in the Old Testament. Punishment was only ever applicable when people had done wrong, knew it and understood its purpose. Failure to discipline appropriately in childhood could result in problems in later life. The writer/editor of 1 Kings has an intriguing aside on the behaviour of David's son Adonijah. His attempt to become king is put down at least in part to his father's earlier failure to offer him suitable discipline and guidance. Clearly the writer of Kings saw this parental failure as noteworthy (1 Kings 1:5ff). If a child grew up in a totally unruly way then the parents, together, could take very drastic action, along with the wider community (Deuteronomy 21:18ff). This particular passage may cause us to wince and wonder, but at least it does show us the seriousness with which a failure to observe the fifth commandment was taken.

Great care should be taken in applying all of this today. The basic principle seems clear: children need discipline provided in the context of loving relationships. Discipline will always therefore have as its main concern the growth of the child towards self-discipline through being given reasonable boundaries appropriate to their age and development. This will mean the use of punishment only as a final sanction and will certainly avoid violence and abuse of the child in any way. It does mean that there is a right place for boundary setting, correction and rebuke where necessary, but always out of love for the child. It needs to acknowledge that very often 'bad' behaviour by a child arises from a lack of self-worth, lack of security and love. Unacceptable behaviour in these circumstances is not necessarily deliberate and may be a cry for help. So great wisdom is needed in working with any children to ensure that discipline is loving and appropriate to the child and the circumstances. Whatever the situation no physical forms of punishment should ever be used in Christian clubs, camps or the like; if punishment really does become necessary then some other form of sanction will need to be found, such as withdrawal of a privilege or temporary exclusion from a much-loved activity.

To fail to discipline is, at root, to fail to love. But God's endless loving grace wanting the very best for his children is the root from which all our discipline must grow.

Combining all of this together gives us a pattern of teaching in which the faith story of God's people is faithfully and regularly retold alongside the Law and the lessons of life experience. The motivating force behind all such teaching was the gracious love of God himself. Discipline was included as part of this love. The whole teaching process was grounded in lives which modelled living under the rule of God and was done through a variety of means including one which deserves its own separate treatment; that is, participation in worship.

5 WORSHIP

Throughout the Old Testament children participate in the corporate worship of Israel. They ate the Passover in Egypt (Exodus 12) and are mentioned as important participants in all subsequent celebrations of this feast. They would have lived out in the temporary shelters of the Feast of Booths along with the whole family (Leviticus 23:42), joined in the celebrations on the Day of Atonement (Leviticus 16) and week by week shared in the remembrance of and celebration of the Sabbath. Children were, then, part of the community at worship. We know from the Gospels that Jesus himself as a child was part of his own community at worship (Luke 2:4ff and 4:16). It seems that as part of their participation it was to be expected that children would have questions that needed answering. Such questioning was not regarded as an expression of doubt or faithlessness but as an opportunity for further recall of God's dealings with his people. No doubt the children sang, clapped, and danced during the various ceremonies along with everyone else. Because they belonged to God's people they were expected to celebrate with all of God's people. Such participation was a crucial part of their lives both as an expression of their belonging and as part of their learning. It took place both in the home and amongst the wider community. Today it remains just as important that children are allowed to experience and join in with the worship of God's people, for they will learn and sense that they belong through such active involvement. However, for children from non-church families we will always need to be aware of how strange and unnatural worship may at first appear to be.

Within the believing community worship is vital, but for outreach to children from beyond that community, at least in the early stages, it may prove to be inappropriate and even irrelevant.

AND SO TO JESUS

It is against this background of the Old Testament that we must take both the life and teaching of Jesus himself to which we must turn next. But before we do so let us summarise our survey of children in the Old Testament as follows:

1 Children are full human beings, not humans in the making. As such they both bear the image of God and are caught up in human sinfulness.

2 God gives children to parents and the wider community as gifts of his creativity. It is the responsibility of the parents and that wider community, therefore, in loving, thankful response, to care for all children.

3 Such care will be expressed through providing food, clothing, shelter and health. It will also include sharing the story of God's love and action and of his way for living. In other words it will care for the total well-being, the shalom, of each child.

4 The key to this total well-being will be the knowledge of belonging to a people, their history and to their loving, saving Creator and holding fast to his vision of what one day will be.

| ACTIVITIES |

1 Take time to go through each section reading the passages and reflecting on them. Are the conclusions reached valid? If not, what do you think are valid conclusions?

2 What implications might these conclusions have for your work with children?

| **FURTHER READING** |

A Theology of Children's Ministry (edition entitled *Children's Ministry* in Australia), Lawrence Richards, Zondervan, 1983

JESUS AND THE CHILDREN

Jesus of Nazareth did not live or teach in an historical vacuum. He was clearly a first-century Jew. His teaching and life-style were firmly based on the scriptures and offered within the world of a nation under Roman occupation. We need to look at his life and teaching with regard to children in this context. This will actually help us in the long run because we too have to work out the teaching of the scriptures in our own particular historical context.

JESUS THE CHILD

The fact that the eternal Son of God should become human is a staggering and glorious truth. That the New Testament does not tell us a great deal about how this worked out in the early years is perhaps one of the great mysteries of what is and is not in the Bible. But the little information we do have is very valuable.

The truth of the incarnation is a massive affirmation of being human. All the truths about value and dignity that we noticed in the early chapters of Genesis are reaffirmed by Jesus taking on human flesh. He has now himself been through the whole process of foetal growth, birth, infancy, childhood, puberty and early adulthood. He knows what it is like to cry in hunger, learn to walk and talk and so on. Luke's Gospel shows that Jesus went through the same process of growing up that all humans have to go through. In that sense he has further hallowed every stage of human birth, development and growth to maturity.

It is interesting to note the particular ways in which Jesus' growth is described. 'And the child grew and became strong; he was filled with wisdom, and the grace of God was upon him.' And 'Jesus grew in wisdom and stature, and in favour with God and men' (Luke 2:40 and 52). Let's take the different aspects of growth one by one.

1 PHYSICAL GROWTH

We do not know Jesus' final height, build or particular distinguishing features, but what we do know is that just like every other human being he went through the process of physical development. He had to learn to sit, stand, walk etc. He went through all the bodily changes associated with puberty and finally reached his adult height.

2 INTELLECTUAL AND MENTAL GROWTH

Jesus did not arrive in the world with all the knowledge of heaven stored away in his brain; if he had he would not have been fully human. He had to learn to talk, to name things, to know how to use things. He had to learn the scriptures just like all his contemporaries and his own younger brothers and sisters. He was clearly a very intelligent child, as the incident in the temple illustrates (Luke 2:41–52), but he had to learn just like everyone else. Note that his intellectual growth was not simply in knowledge but in applying that knowledge, ie in wisdom. His wise teaching as an adult was arrived at through his years of listening to and pondering on the scriptures, from his prayer life and his accumulated learning from life. This learning occurred primarily in the context of his shared home life, his life in the local community as a child and young adult, and then in the period of his ministry in the community of the twelve. (Note that this community included women as well as men – see Luke 8:1ff.) Certainly Jesus also spent much time alone with his Father, but to emphasise this to the exclusion of the great time spent within the community is to present a very imbalanced picture. Jesus' learning drawn from scripture, prayer and life experience needs to be seen as an interwoven pattern: life experiences in the home and community raising questions about scripture, and scripture raising questions and helping Jesus to understand the life experiences – all infused with prayerful conversation with the Father both alone and as part of the community's corporate prayer life.

3 SPIRITUAL GROWTH

The phrase 'grew in favour with God' does not mean that Jesus was less favoured by the Father when he was young and more favoured as he grew up. If it meant this it would make a nonsense of the earlier phrase 'the grace of God was upon him' and the whole thrust of the infancy narratives. What it does imply is a development in Jesus' grasp of his knowledge of the Father. The temple incident shows that Jesus' understanding of the Father and of his own relationship to him was quite extraordinary for his age. But he is also learning through listening and asking questions of the elders. He could not at this stage have undertaken his later ministry; he still had too much to learn, experience and understand. Some may find this difficult to accept, thinking that it implies less than perfection in the eternal Son of God. It does not. Perhaps the simplest way of putting it is this: Jesus as a three year old was all that a three year old should be; at twelve he was all that a twelve year old should be. But he was a real three year old with all the limits of that age, and likewise at twelve and throughout his life.

4 SOCIAL GROWTH

Jesus grew in favour with people as well. He developed relationships and friendships within the community in which he grew up. He was part of the community of Nazareth; he attended synagogue regularly, worked alongside his father, Joseph, as a carpenter and lived as a carpenter until he was around thirty years old. He had younger brothers and sisters and was aware of a wider family network through Aunt Elizabeth and his rather oddball cousin John. Jesus developed the abilities of conversation, befriending, guiding, communicating etc, which he displayed in the years of his public ministry, in the hubbub of life in Nazareth; apparently not the kind of community that many anticipated would produce great leaders or teachers (John 1:46).

5 EMOTIONAL GROWTH

Whilst this is not specifically referred to in Luke's Gospel we can be sure that it happened. That the emotions Jesus expressed as an adult – such as compassion for the hungry and helpless crowd, tears at the graveside of Lazarus, and desire for the support of others in

Gethsemane, and the anguish on the cross – could have been so deep and appropriate shows that he developed emotionally to the full. To be able to handle such emotions so fully and perfectly in his adulthood, Jesus must have experienced real developments in his emotional life as a child and young adult.

So Jesus grew up, just like everyone else. If he went through growth and development in this way then surely we should accept that this really is the way God intended it. We should take all aspects of human development seriously.

We need to add one more key point to this picture of Jesus growing up. The most important people in Jesus' development were his parents. Mary fed him, changed him, weaned him. Together with Joseph she helped him learn to walk and talk. They would have shared with him the stories of God's dealings with Israel down the ages and taught him the Law; they had him circumcised to show he belonged to God's covenant people. They took him to the synagogue and celebrated the Sabbath and festivals with him. Probably they sent him to the synagogue school to be taught and learn the Law and Wisdom at the instruction of the scribes. At some point they presumably shared the story of his birth. They therefore had a crucial role to play in helping their son understand his true identity and purpose, although they did not know how that would work out in detail. Joseph also taught Jesus everything he knew about carpentry. At thirteen Jesus officially entered adulthood and when, as it seems right to assume, Joseph died, he would have taken up the family business and duties as the eldest son until the time came for him to begin his public ministry. Mary's influence was clearly very strong; notice the role she still plays at the outset of Jesus' ministry at the wedding in Cana. There was to be a painful separation as Jesus' ministry developed, and his brothers at least thought he had gone off his head, but up to the age of thirty Jesus was obedient to his parents and lived at home as the expression of his obedience to his Father God. When Jesus hung on the cross as the perfect sacrifice for the sins of the world, it was his perfection as a child, eldest son, community member, and carpenter that made him acceptable, just as much as the perfection of his three year's public ministry.

JESUS AND CHILDREN – THE EVENTS

The rabbis of Jesus time were not oblivious to children. The Mishnah (an early collection of Jewish writings) tells us of the debates they had about when a child could first sin. There are even references to rabbis playing with children. But by and large children were regarded only as significant in the context of education. By the first century BC more formal education in the Law had become established and was given great importance. Children continued to be seen as a gift from God, belonging to the covenant people, but apart from teaching the Law the rabbis basically had nothing to do with children.

Compared with the prevailing attitudes of the Roman world this was a very positive view of children. In Roman thinking children were at times idealised but also they were regarded as disposable. The horrific practice of exposure (leaving a child out to die) in the Roman world is well attested: a practice definitely not copied by the Jews.

Jesus clearly reflects more of his own Jewish background than that of the ruling power in his land. But his vision of God's kingdom means that he actually responds to and views children in a whole new way. Just as he treated women with a dignity they had not experienced before, so too his treatment of children was radically new.

1 OBSERVING

Jesus, it seems, was a great observer of children. Matthew and Luke both recall Jesus' use of an incident of children at play in the market place to illustrate how people had reacted to John the Baptist and himself (Matthew 11:16ff and Luke 7:32). He is aware of the children being brought by their parents, and of the child standing close by during a discussion with the disciples (Matthew 19:13ff and 18:1ff). He is aware of children. His use of the market place games also shows that he had a fully realistic view of children; there is no idealisation of them here. What there is is an awareness of a lesson to be drawn from their behaviour which applies to all ages.

2 WELCOMING

We noted above that outside the formal educational setting Jewish rabbis basically had little time for children. It is no great surprise therefore to find the disciples of rabbi Jesus trying to turn away the parents and their children when they seek the Teacher's blessing (Matthew 19:13–15, Mark 10:13–16, Luke 18:15–17). The surprise is Jesus' indignation against the disciples for their action. The word Mark uses for 'indignant' is a very strong one and is used only here in the Gospels. He was furious with them for trying to keep the children away! What he then does is to go way beyond even the probable expectations of the people who actually brought these children. (Note the text does not state whether it was parents or older brothers and sister, the two most likely groups to have brought children, or other adults – it simply says 'people'.) Rabbis were known to offer blessings to children at the Day of Atonement, but such blessings would have been with respect to the child's future. Jesus rather gives them a *current* value and status and expresses this by physically embracing them. They are not promised the kingdom in the future, they are told it belongs to them at that precise moment; in grace God has already chosen to give them his kingdom.

So often this incident and that recorded in Matthew 18:2 are depicted in highly sentimental terms. 'Isn't it lovely the way Jesus places his hands on them and blesses them.' What Jesus does is quite incredible; this is no simple pat on the head, the taking in the arms is the symbolic embrace of welcome by the Messiah. It is akin to the father's embrace of his returning son in Luke 15. It places the children within the kingdom there and then; not waiting to enter it sometime when they are older.

3 TEACHING

Children were clearly part of the crowds on at least some of the occasions when Jesus was teaching. They were present at the feeding of the 5000; indeed it was a child who gave his 'packed lunch' to Jesus to use (John 6:9). The incident we have referred to in Mark 10 also includes teaching which some of the children themselves would have understood. (Some at least were too young: Luke uses the word for babies.) But on no occasion do we find Jesus teaching children on their own. They may be part of the larger crowd, or even of a smaller group, but the teaching is always primarily for the adults who are there. This surely implies that Jesus basically endorsed his own experience and the pattern of the Law. It is the responsibility of parents and the household to teach children.

4 HEALING

Several of Jesus' recorded miracles involve children. There is the Canaanite or Syro-Phoenician woman's daughter (Matthew 15:21ff, Mark 7:24ff); the demoniac boy (Matthew 17:14ff, Mark 9:14ff, Luke 9:37ff); Jairus' daughter (Matthew 9:18ff, Mark 5:21ff, Luke 8:41ff); and the official's son (John 4:46ff). Clearly if a child needed healing, Jesus was willing to offer it. But we can notice several things about these incidents. In the first two the problem is demonic. Clearly children can be affected by the demonic and its manifestations can be very unpleasant. In the other two cases Jesus is dealing with very serious illnesses; he does not simply heal a minor complaint but rescues both from the jaws of death. In all four cases however we should note that the request to Jesus comes from the parents not the children themselves. Jesus heals in response to the parent's request and faith; nothing is said on any of the occasions regarding the child's faith, the children simply receive from Jesus. It is perhaps worth adding that the four 'families' cover quite a range of social background and standing as well as religious affiliation.

5 WORSHIP

When Jesus enters Jerusalem on what is now commonly called Palm Sunday there were plenty of children in the crowd. They were up in Jerusalem for the Passover along with their families, just as Jesus had been when he was younger. These children waved palms and cheered themselves hoarse for Jesus. When this cheering was taken up in the temple courtyard it simply became all too much for the religious authorities who called on Jesus to stop them. Jesus point blank refuses to do so. Instead he endorses the worship and adoration not only of these children but of the reality of children's worship more widely (Matthew 21:1ff).

JESUS AND CHILDREN – THE TEACHING

In looking at the way Jesus welcomed children we noticed the link between his actions and his words. The two reinforce each other. It is important to look more closely at the teaching in which Jesus mentions children. These passages have caused a great deal of debate over the years and it is beyond the scope of this book to go into that debate in great detail. (See Further Reading for some of the key books.) Some thoughts, however, are essential.

The key passages in question are Matthew 18:1–14 (and the parallel passages in Mark 9:33–37, Luke 9:46–48; 15:4–7) and Matthew 19:13–15 (and the parallels in Mark 10:13–16, Luke 18:15–17).

1 MATTHEW 18 AND PARALLELS

Matthew 18:2ff seems straightforward enough. Jesus uses the child to make a point to the adult disciples. But what is it about the child that they need to become like? How is the child humble? The most obvious answer seems to lie in the commonly accepted status, or rather lack of it, given to children in that society. Children were viewed as the least important; they are in the lowliest position available. But the child has not put himself in that position, he is simply there; the disciples, on the other hand, have to opt to place themselves as servants, as the lowliest. The implication of Matthew's words has to be that this child, by virtue of being in the lowly place, is already great in the kingdom. This is not because the child is innocent or sinless (that would be counter to the Old Testament) but because God graciously chooses to give the kingdom to the lowly, the least important, the poor. The following words concerning welcoming a child are paralleled in Mark and Luke. Here it is clear that Jesus is placing immense value on every child; his followers are to welcome children just as they have seen their master do. 'In my name' does not refer to the children, as some have sought to suggest, but to the people doing the welcoming. Children are to be welcomed on the basis of Jesus' person and character; such welcoming implies care and concern for the children. It is similar in nature to the injunction to welcome the hungry in Matthew 25:31ff. To welcome the child is to welcome Jesus himself.

What follows in Matthew may or may not refer to children. The change to the use of 'little ones' could well imply a change in thought away from children as such towards those who have made themselves little for the sake of the kingdom. This would make sense of the initial entrance of the child as a living visual aid for Jesus. The prime purpose of the passage is not to teach about children themselves but about greatness in the kingdom. Anything that we do learn about children (such as their desire to be near Jesus and their vulnerability) is effectively an added bonus.

2 MATTHEW 19 AND PARALLELS

'The kingdom of God belongs to such as these.' One thing in this phrase is quite clear; children have a place in the kingdom (rule/reign) of God. You cannot keep them out of it by saying they are not yet old enough, because they don't understand properly, or whatever other excuse could be given. No child is too young for the kingdom.

What is not quite so clear is whether we should understand this phrase to mean that all children are part of the kingdom because they are children, or that children are being used here again as a living visual aid of how the kingdom is entered; you receive it, you do not earn it. The arguments used for the different interpretations involve detailed analysis of the Greek text and debate about how it would have been said in Jesus' native Aramaic. I have to say that often the entrenched positions that have been taken up over this debate may have produced plenty of learned papers but have not helped develop mutual listening and respect for differing views. Could it just be that we need to hold different understandings in tension? If this is done then an understanding along the following lines develops.

The kingdom is a gift of God; it is given in grace. Yet like all gifts to be enjoyed, it must be received – and it can be rejected. God chooses to give the kingdom to children. He does this not because they are innocent or because they deserve it but because in his sheer grace he wants the 'poor in spirit', the lowly, to have the kingdom. Children in the very nature of their vulnerability are lowly, so he gives them the kingdom. Those who are not children, which in Jesus' day meant everyone aged twelve or thirteen and over, need to learn from this that the kingdom is a gift of grace; it is not earned and is enjoyed simply by receiving it just as the children have received Jesus.

As if to emphasise the contrast of the ease with which the child receives the kingdom and the difficulty of an adult learning from them, all three gospel writers immediately follow this incident and saying with the story of the rich young ruler. In each account Jesus is recorded as saying, 'How hard it is for a rich man to enter the kingdom of God.' There is the ease of receiving like children, but actually for a rich, clean-living, morally upstanding young man to receive the kingdom is just too costly. He cannot cope with taking up the lowly position of dispensing with all his worldly standing and following Jesus. The children were in the privileged position; they had nothing to lose but everything to gain: the rich young man has, in one sense, to lose everything in order to gain everything. No wonder it was hard for him but easy for the children!

CONCLUSIONS

If the various passages are placed together alongside the events that were examined earlier certain overall conclusions can be drawn.

1   Jesus has reinforced the value of humanity by becoming human himself. This is obviously shown further by the redemptive work of his death on the cross. By going through the whole process of human growth and development he has shown us that this is God's pattern for all humanity. This being the case we ignore the reality and lessons of human development at our peril.

2   Jesus, in his ministry, has placed a very high value and dignity on children. He was prepared to go against the conventions and attitudes of his own culture and era in order to do this. He thus reinforced the value built into creation itself.

3   Jesus also acknowledged the vulnerable position of children and expressed God's love and grace towards them because of this.

4   Jesus welcomed children to be near him, cared for their needs and showed that they belonged within the realm of God's loving rule.

5   Jesus endorsed the role of parents and the wider community in

the care of children. Apparently he never worked with children in isolation from their wider context.

In short: children mattered to Jesus. They therefore must matter to his followers.

| ACTIVITIES |

1 As with Chapter 2, go back over the sections of this chapter and read the references. Are the conclusions valid? If not, what are your conclusions?

2 In what way do these modify the conclusions you reached after Chapter 2, if at all?

3 What implications do the conclusions from Chapters 2 and 3 have for the way you work with children?

| FURTHER READING |

Children and God, Ron Buckland, Scripture Union, 1988
Jesus and the Children, Hans Reudi Weber, World Council of Churches, 1979

A Theology of Children's Ministry (edition entitled *Children's Ministry* in Australia), Lawrence Richards, Zondervan, 1983

'NOT ON THEIR OWN?'

The talk, entitled 'The Spiritual Life of Children', had come to its end and the speaker allowed time for some questions. As is often the case there was a slightly embarrassed silence, then suddenly one person spoke up; 'That's all very interesting, but what's it got to do with my midweek club and the kids who come to it?' A very fair and proper question. One which is equally appropriate at this point in this book.

The rightness of the question lies in a deep concern for actually getting on with the task of sharing God's love with children today. What sadly often lies behind it is also a lack of desire to really allow our lives to be shaped by the teaching of the scriptures. It should never be a case of either modern practice or wrestling with scripture but always a case of 'both/and'. So if the temptation is to think that what has been said so far does not have a great deal to do with the midweek club, or whatever, hang in there – it does!

EVANGELISM

When Jesus commissioned his followers to go into all the world he did not place any exclusion clauses on the command. They were to go to all nations and be witnesses for Jesus (Matthew 28:18–20). Their task was not simply to seek conversions but to see people becoming real disciples, that is learners, of Jesus. At its most straightforward this must surely mean that the Good News of Jesus is to be made known to children as well as adults. They are part of all nations; part of the whole creation.

Then as we read through Acts and the letters of the New Testament it seems clear that children were included within the life of the new covenant communities.

1   On the Day of Pentecost Peter declares that the promise and gift of the Holy Spirit is not simply for the immediate hearers but also for their children. By children Peter probably had descendants in mind rather than simply his hearers' immediate offspring, but children are clearly included.

2   There are the stories of the conversion of whole households (Acts 10 and 11; 16:25–34; 18:8, 1 Corinthians 1:16). In these households there would have been the head of the household, his wife, children, servants or slaves and their children as well. It is surely beyond belief to suggest that there were never any children in any of these households given the knowledge we have of the make up of households throughout the Roman Empire at that time.

3   Paul specifically refers to and writes to children in two of his letters (Ephesians 6:1ff, Colossians 3:20ff). This implies two things. First, children were normally present as part of the worshipping community in these two places. Second, that if they were present Paul expected them to listen to the whole letter, not only the bits referring to them. This has the consequence that all the teaching about relationships, for example, is applicable to behaviour in the family. It is not only a question of 'obeying parents'.

This inclusion of children in the new covenant makes logical sense. The new Jewish Christians were used to the idea that their children belonged inside God's covenant and Jesus had refocused this by his own actions and teaching. Hence we should expect that they would include children in the new covenant community and teach Gentiles who become believers to do the same.

It also accords with the message of forgiveness and reconciliation through Jesus' death and resurrection that was proclaimed by the early church. Paul makes it abundantly clear that all people are caught up in sin and under God's judgment; all are in need of forgiveness. There are no exclusions for children in Romans 3. Children, in this sense, need God's saving grace as much as anyone. The glory is that God's love has reached out and brought about complete forgiveness and new life through the death of his Son Jesus. This act of grace is for children as well as adults.

For all these reasons we can, I believe, safely conclude that the early church included children within the scope of their evangelistic and discipling task. But on all the evidence we have this was done in the context of the children's wider family/community. We never read of children being evangelised on their own.

On the face of it then the answer to the question, 'Should we evangelise children today?' is very simple. Yes!

Yet to leave it as such a bald affirmative is to avoid the hard questions which are being asked in many quarters about the rightness or appropriateness of evangelising children today. Indeed it is also to ignore the wider lessons learnt about children from the Old Testament, Jesus and the actual practice of evangelism that is found in the New Testament.

In the remainder of this chapter we will deal with the first 'hard question': namely, 'Should we evangelise children on their own?' In the next chapter we will look at the question, 'Are children too young to be evangelised?

'SHOULD WE EVANGELISE CHILDREN ON THEIR OWN?'

There are many from both within and outside the church who argue that because children are part of a wider family and are the responsibility primarily of their parents it is wrong to seek to evangelise them as a separate group or as individuals apart from the family. In the light of what we have seen in the Old Testament, Jesus' own actions and teaching, and the continued key role of parents in the New Testament there seems to be much validity in this argument. Under God it *is* parents who are primarily responsible for the spiritual, as well as the physical, well-being of their children. If we are to be true to the scriptures, surely we should not seek to usurp that role? On the other hand it is quite clear that for many children in Western societies the wider family network has broken down – there may be only one parent regularly around, and for many community life has also broken down. This leaves large numbers of children from a very early age being left largely to their own devices. However much we may be saddened by this or argue that it is not in the children's best interests it is the context in which we are now working with children. There is always a severe danger of overplaying this line. The vast majority of children *are* being raised in homes where they are loved, wanted and cared for to the best of their parents' ability. This goes for children from all social classes, ethnic backgrounds, and whether there are one or two parents in the home. If we put the whole picture together I would suggest that we rightly seek to share the Good News of Jesus with children, but wherever and whenever possible we do so in the context of their family and wider community. If we do not we could easily be in danger of undermining the role of the parents and even placing the child under undue pressures.

ROGER'S STORY

Let's illustrate the dangers of working with the child in isolation through an imaginary story based on real-life experiences.

Roger is nine. His parents only ever go near church for weddings and funerals but encourage Roger to go to the midweek club run by the church down the street. They do this so that he can make friends with other children his age and because they feel they ought to be able to trust church people with their son. However, he now seems to be taking the 'religious' bit rather more seriously. They find him reading his Bible at night sometimes, and he keeps asking if he can go to church on a Sunday morning. Usually they don't do much on Sundays except for the occasional visit to Roger's grandparents. They have never really bothered to find out what happens at the club or church and no one from church has ever been to see them. As Roger appears to become more 'religious' so his parents become increasingly uneasy, especially when he comes home one evening very upset. Eventually they discover from him that he is scared because of something said in the club by one of the leaders. He is upset that his parents will be 'going to hell' because they are not Christians, and Roger cannot decide whether he would rather be in heaven with Jesus and the club leaders or in hell with Mum, Dad and his grandparents. Understandably the parents themselves become very upset with the club leaders and telephone one of them to express their anger. The club leader 'helpfully' tells them, 'Roger is quite right. You will be in hell if you do not become Christians.' After a sharp intake of breath by Roger's mother the leader continues, 'Yes, I know that this is a hard truth to accept but you and Roger have got to come to terms with it sooner or later.' Roger's Mum slammed the phone down. Next week Roger chooses not to go to the club. Nor the week after that. The leaders pray for him and his parents but they never see any of them again.

This particular scenario is an imaginary one but it points up genuine problems. By working with Roger without any reference to or contact with his wider family the club leaders have created a conflict between the child and the parents. They have presented the child with an apparent choice of monumental proportions; Jesus or parents; heaven or hell. They have made stark judgments about parents whom they have never met or talked to. And when they do have a belated chance to talk they are downright rude, showing no hint of compassion or concern at having upset Roger. Then they make no effort to help Roger in the long run; have they consigned him to hell also for siding with his parents rather than with Jesus?

How different the story might be if from the very outset the local church had sought to work with Roger's whole family. As Roger joined the club why didn't any leader visit the home soon after? Why weren't the parents invited to come along one week and watch or join in all of the activities? Why weren't special events arranged for all the family to join in together? And suppose all of this had been done but the parents had shown little or no interest. When Roger begins to show a deeper interest in spiritual matters, why aren't the parents visited again to talk this over with them to suggest ways in which they might help Roger with this new interest that he has? And why hadn't far more care been taken over the teaching content and language being used? Suppose, even, that it reaches the situation of the telephone call; why doesn't the leader listen carefully and offer to come round and talk with the whole family? And when Roger does not reappear, why no visit?

If the parents really do have a key role to play, surely those who work with children should seek to work as partners with those parents wherever possible, whether or not the parents profess faith in Christ for themselves.

YASMIN'S STORY

If one were to consider a situation involving a child being brought up in a family from another major faith then the questions become even more sharply focused. Another imaginary story based on real life experiences may help us see this.

Yasmin is ten. Her family are Muslims. Every day after school Yasmin attends the mosque to be taught the Qur'an and Arabic. Her parents are less devout than her paternal grandparents who live with them, but they believe that Islam is important to their own identity and infinitely preferable to the immoral world around them. Through a school friend Yasmin hears about a holiday club being run by the local Baptist church. (Note that she has no idea what 'Baptist' means.) Her parents agree to her attending because her friend has been allowed to go and the leaflet Yasmin has brought home makes it look like a good way to spend a week of her holidays. They are quite happy that there will be Bible stories as they believe it will be good for her to learn some of these and they do not feel it will be a threat to her Islamic faith. The grandfather is not so sure but is overruled. Yasmin is enthralled by the stories of Jesus that she hears; especially the healings and the way Jesus treats people. She does not understand some things because they seem to differ from what she has been taught at the mosque (especially about Jesus' death), but she wants to find out more. The leader of the club is a single man in his twenties. He suggests that she starts coming along to the weekly midweek club held in the church for children her age. She asks her parents. Now the grandfather becomes very concerned and says so. Is Yasmin going to stop attending the mosque? Can we trust this young man? Is this church trying to break up our family? What will the Mullah say? As the conversation unfolds more weird and wonderful fears are expressed including recollections of how Christians had treated Muslims in the Crusades.

These are genuine fears and anxieties felt by members of other faiths (not just Islam) about any member of their family being 'taken away from them' by the activities of Christians. In this case we could be creating tensions and difficulties for a ten-year-old girl with which she would not be able to cope.

How much better if alongside welcoming Yasmin to the holiday club and inviting her to an ongoing club (a far better option in itself than a church service) the organisers had all along been seeking to befriend and work alongside the whole of Yasmin's family. A woman rather than a young man would have been the main contact with Yasmin and the young man would have worked with boys and men. The local church should be building bridges of friendship with the members of other faith communities out of a real love for their well-being and a desire to develop a just community. In this process dialogue will inevitably occur in which the differences of the faiths and the real love of God will be made known. Jesus will be shared with individual members of a family, and the family as a whole. But it will be done in a way which, so far as is possible, does not create tensions for a child with which they themselves are not ready to cope.

It may become a different story in a few years time for Yasmin. As a teenager disaffected with her parents' faith and yet not happy with the secular ungodly world around her, she may decide that she really does want to follow Christ. This could create a major division within her family. In this event the local church would have to offer her all the support it could whilst still seeking to work with her whole family.

It is here that we would have to take seriously Jesus' teaching regarding higher loyalties than family (Matthew 8:18–22; 10:34–39; 12:46–50). At the end of the day the gospel can divide families as well as unite them. Loyalty to God and his rule has to be placed above loyalty to the human family. But this should never be at the expense of continuing to love and care for that human family so far as they allow us to do so (Mark 7:1–13, John 19:26ff). Anyone who becomes a follower of Christ commits themselves to honouring their father and mother, as Jesus himself did, even when they may choose to cut us off because of our commitment to Jesus.

CONCLUSIONS

So where does this leave us? I believe that it does allow us, in response to both the 'Great Commission' (Matthew 28:18ff) and the two 'Great Commandments' (Luke 10:25ff), to share the Good News of Jesus with children of all ages from whatever background they may come. But we must do so in ways which are above suspicion and which seek, so far as is possible, to share the Good News with the child's whole family. This will mean a greater emphasis in local churches on community and family evangelism. (This will be the subject of Chapter 7.)

It will mean a complete openness with parents and carers about both the content of the story of Jesus that we share and the methods which we use with children. This is summarised well in *All God's Children?*

We should seek to evangelise children in a spirit of coming alongside their parents rather than that of coming against them. Several guidelines should help this to happen.

1 Only share with children what you can share with their parents.
2 Encourage children to tell their parents what they have done or learned or care about.
3 Do not encourage a 'defiant spirit' – a feeling of superiority in the child over his parents because he is, or is becoming, a Christian.
4 Keep a steady flow of information to the parents.
5 Set up family opportunities – outings, parent's evenings etc.
6 Always seek parental support and approval.
(*All God's Children*, p 44)

In short, it will be a relationship-based evangelism both with the children themselves and their wider family. As such it will need to involve the whole local church community rather than the dedicated isolated individual.

| ACTIVITIES |

1 Use either Roger or Yasmin's story and discuss how you would have handled the situation.

2 What practical ways can you think of building relationships with the wider family?

| FURTHER READING |

All God's Children?, General Synod Board of Education and Board of Mission, National Society/ Church House Publishing, 1991

Family: The Vital Factor, Moira Eastman, Collins Dove (Australia), 1989

'TOO YOUNG FOR GOD?'

'But Mummy, why can't I watch that programme?' asked the seven year old desperate to see his hero Lenny Henry. 'You're too young, dear. You wouldn't enjoy it.' Mum actually meant, 'There are scenes and language in it that I do not think it would be good for you to see and hear,' but that was going to be too difficult to explain. Most people believe that there is knowledge and experience which it is inappropriate for children to have. The older the child grows the less this becomes the case, though it is not simply a matter of age; emotional stability, mental comprehension and other factors will also be brought into play. Consider, for example, the deep concern about violent and pornographic videos being watched by very young children. We know it is happening and there are very few voices suggesting it is anything other than damaging to those children's development. It is possible for children to have too much, too soon. By their very nature children are too young for some things.

This raises the question of children's evangelism. Are children too young to be evangelised? Is it more than they can cope with? Is asking them to make decisions about Jesus beyond their current abilities? Or is, perhaps, 'evangelism' the wrong word to use in dealing with children? We began to touch on this in the previous chapter; in this chapter we must examine the question in greater detail.

Once again the questions are clearly valid. A child of three or four finds it hard enough to choose what clothes to wear in the morning or what cereals to eat for breakfast. By the time they are seven or eight there is no problem with such choices, but most of us would not expect them to be able to choose their life's career with any great certainty, nor would we necessarily want them to. Their experience is limited and so are their abilities to make such choices. The way in which their minds work, they make moral choices or handle relationships have all changed markedly from when they were only three, but we all know that they will undergo further radical changes in the following years, particularly through and beyond adolescence. So can we really expect children to make choices about faith which we believe are of eternal consequence? Should we not leave it at least until the teenage years?

But if we do that are we not in danger of both ignoring the experience of many in the past and failing to value children for themselves in the present? The stories of children experiencing God in a deep and meaningful way which subsequently shapes the rest of their lives are numerous. This is true from the general work available on religious experience (note especially Robert Coles' splendid book *The Spiritual Life of Children*) and from the specifically Christian testimonies of many adults who recall encountering Jesus for themselves in childhood, even as young as two or three. In the scriptures we should note the stories of Samuel, Naaman's young servant girl and Jesus himself at the age of twelve, to see that children can and do have very real knowledge and experience of God for themselves. To deny this would be to underplay scripture and the testimony of history and experience. It would be to limit children unfairly.

So if we are content to say that children can have real experiences of God and respond to him in meaningful, even life-changing ways, what do we make of the equally true limitations and question marks raised earlier? To begin to answer this question let us return to the lessons we noted from the Bible in Chapters 2 and 3.

HUMAN BEINGS EXPERIENCE DEVELOPMENT

We noted that God has always intended that human beings go through the process of growth and development. It is part of his creative plan that we experience the womb, birth, infancy, childhood, adolescence etc. He has further endorsed and hallowed this process by going through it himself in the incarnation of Jesus. That there is a growth process built into this which is not simply physical but also mental, moral and spiritual is noted regularly through scripture by the references (both literal and metaphorical) made to infancy and childhood in the prophets, wisdom literature and New Testament letters (eg Proverbs 20:11; 22:6, Isaiah 7:14ff; 11:6–9, Hosea 11:1–4, 1 Corinthians 13:11; 14:20, Hebrews 5:11–14). This is in addition to the specific references about Samuel's, John the Baptist's and Jesus' own human development.

Given all this I have always been disturbed by the negative way in which many Christians have approached the work of social scientists and psychologists. If the social sciences are about studying human behaviour so that we are better able to understand how and why human beings behave and develop in the ways they do, are we not basically studying the way God has made us (and the impact of human sinfulness). If psychologists, through their study, can throw light onto how our minds work and develop as we grow up, I strongly believe that we should take serious note of this in the ways in which we work with people.

We should always seek both to view in the light of scripture any theories which are developed and to note the provisional nature of such theories (however ardently they are put forward as the answer!). But having done so we must use those insights of such studies that seem true and useful.

So what lessons should we be aware of in our work with children which will help us to answer the questions with which we opened the chapter?

THE WAY CHILDREN THINK

When writing to the Christians at Corinth Paul acknowledges that his own thinking has developed. In particular he writes of his childhood and says, 'I thought like a child, reasoned like a child' (1 Corinthians 13:11). So he was aware that our thinking and reasoning processes *do* develop from childhood into adulthood. He was not a modern developmental psychologist but his own self-awareness helps us view modern work on how such reasoning processes develop in a positive light.

The Swiss psychologist Jean Piaget's studies raised many questions about the mental and intellectual capacity and development of children. These studies have been subsequently modified by others. However, the consensus of all work is that there are limitations in the way children think. As an example we may consider the thought patterns typical of children between six or seven and ten or twelve as suggested by Piaget. During these years children think in 'concrete' rather than 'abstract' terms. In other words they think in solid facts and stories rather than in the realm of concepts and ideas. Margaret Donaldson has helped redefine this somewhat by showing that in bursts children *do* think in abstract terms, but the younger they are, generally, the less able they are to sustain thinking or apply it in a variety of contexts. In terms of our work with children then it will normally be less helpful to talk, say, in terms of 'sin' as a concept than to talk of specific 'sins' as concrete examples of wrongdoing. It will mean that we will use biblical images that relate more directly to the world of the child; so, for example, it will make more sense to a child to talk in terms of 'being God's friend' (as in Romans 5) rather than being 'born again'. The first picks up on the child's experiences of friendship whilst the second involves a concept which is very hard for a child to imagine. (It proved conceptually too hard for a learned Jewish adult – see John 3.)

'Concrete' thinking will also mean that children will tend to understand our words in a literal form; so some at least will find talk of 'inviting Jesus into your heart' as rather strange because they know where their heart is and that it pumps the blood around your body. It certainly does not sound a nice place for someone as special as Jesus to live.

Children take a long while to develop any sense of history. So Abraham, David, Jesus and Grandad could all well have lived at the same time so far as a young child is concerned. By the time they are eight or nine this historical sense is developing, but even many adults have never fully grasped this one (especially with reference to the Bible, for example where the prophets fit into the history). So we need to take care how we present the stories of scripture. This does not mean that we do not tell the stories at all; but it does mean we take care in *how* we tell them.

The fact, however, that children do have at least flashes of abstract thought will help them and us with the flashes of religious experience that they may have. They will usually be simply accepted by the child as real because they have happened to them. We will rejoice in this and seek to build on it whilst accepting that the child may not be able to 'understand' it at all. This leads us to our next concern.

THE WAY CHILDREN LEARN

A revolution has occurred in school classrooms because of the development of understanding of how children learn. The key elements behind this revolution have been the stress laid on learning by discovery (or active learning) and the importance of learning together. This has led to abandoning the single child working behind their own desk all the time and being taught from the front, and to the introduction of the use of groups of children doing things together and making discoveries as they do so. Such a process of learning, it is argued, in fact applies not only to children but to adults as well. The learning cycle of Experience/Reflection/Understanding/Action has become the prominent educational theory of recent years (see Diagram 1). This is because the traditional model of the teacher telling the pupil centres only on cognitive (mental) learning and it has become clear that learning is far more than a merely mental process; it also involves attitudes and behaviour. Feelings play a key role in all our learning. There is a strong move back towards a primary emphasis on cognitive learning in many circles today, leading to strong calls for a return to more 'traditional' teaching methods. Personally I believe that we need to hold onto a holistic learning model because God is concerned with every part of our beings, not simply our minds. I would encourage us all to continue with active learning methods; the 'school' model for sharing Jesus is far too limited, and Jesus himself certainly did not use it with his disciples.

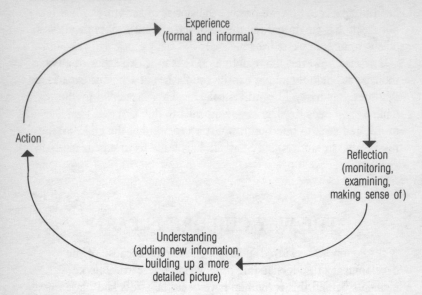

Diagram 1 – The learning cycle

The old Chinese proverb I first heard as a teenager remains very powerful:

> Telling is not teaching,
> Listening is not learning,
> Reading is not studying:
> You learn by doing.

The stress in the scriptures is on 'teaching' children (Deuteronomy 6, Psalm 78, Proverbs 22:6). But a careful look at the most significant passages shows us that although this was sometimes straight input it also included a proper place for visual aids, and children asking questions in response to stories, events, and practices. It used the wisdom of life experience and called on people to reflect on their own experience as well as that of others (especially Proverbs and Ecclesiastes). Teaching also was not always in formal settings. Indeed, arguably it was the increased formalisation of teaching from the Exile onwards that ultimately produced the legalism of Jesus' own day which he so heavily criticised. Jesus' own teaching style was to use parables, lessons from everyday life and experience, and the known scriptures. It was far from being a wholly didactic style. The whole thrust of 'he who has ears to hear let him hear' is an emphasis on the hearer working out the meaning and implications for themselves, rather than being told 'this is what it means'.

I can personally, therefore, see every reason to use active learning methods in our work with both children and adults. There is certainly a place for 'direct input', which with children may mean a short talk. But we will always remember the severe limitations of this as a means of a child really 'getting the gospel into their gut'. It will only ever be one part of the overall jigsaw of learning experiences.

This does have major implications for the way in which we run events for children. It must push us in the direction of using small groups rather than large meetings; active discovery methods with the Bible rather than telling children what a particular story or passage means; in short 'doing things together' in the context of good relationships. It will be an emphasis on learning together through and from experience, as we relate with God together, and through reflection on the scriptures he has given us.

THE WAY CHILDREN CHOOSE

If evangelism is about 'making Jesus known' then it will always involve people in making a choice, or series of choices, at some point, or points. You end up either choosing Jesus or rejecting him. Rejection may well be by neglecting him rather than consciously saying 'No' to him, but it remains rejection at the end of the day (Luke 11:23). If making a choice, or series of choices, about Jesus is a key part in our presentation of the Good News then we need to be clear how, and why, children make choices.

This is highlighted in one particular area of development, namely moral development. How and why do children come to determine right from wrong? Biblically speaking acknowledgement is given to the fact that babies and infants, at least, are incapable of making moral judgments (eg Deuteronomy 1:39, Isaiah 7:14ff, Hebrews

5:13); they will rely entirely on the guidance and direction of adults, especially their parents. But as they are both taught what is right and wrong, develop their own conscience, and from experience learn to distinguish right from wrong they will increasingly be able to make thir own moral choices. This again raises the issue of accountability.

A toddler who likes chocolate biscuits, for example, will almost certainly take one from a plate. Unless they have been told that in their home this is not the way to behave they could not be held to be accountable for a wrong action; if they have been told to wait until they are offered one then they would rightly be told that their action in simply taking one had been wrong. They can only be held accountable for an action when they have been given the guidance to know which is the 'correct' way to behave. This may seem a trivial example but it is a very real one to toddlers! At this stage they are not able to discriminate between a rule which is a household or cultural one, like this example, and a rule which is a divine absolute. Without help and guidance they will never be able to make such a judgment.

Moral judgments throughout childhood will never be entirely independent or individual. The word of parents will be especially strong in the earliest years; as time passes so other authority figures will also have an influence (such as teachers, grandparents, heroes and heroines, and the impersonal TV). Increasingly, however, the norms of the child's peer group will also shape their own moral thinking. Throughout these years there will be a strong sense of right and wrong. Shades of morality only begin to appear with adolescence and the development of more extended abstract thought. 'It's not fair!' is the common cry of the childhood years.

So if children make moral choices largely based on what they have been told, experienced and observed as being right or wrong, and then on what their friends think is right or wrong, it is likely that the same influences will be of real significance when a child comes to make choices about God and what they do or do not believe. In the Holy Spirit's work of bringing about conviction of sin he will normally use the means he has himself built into the processes of life. Hence he will use authority figures, peer groups and individual conscience to highlight the need to be in a right relationship with God. This will often be related to a child's feelings as much as to their thoughts. They will 'feel bad' about going against their parents' ways or stepping out of line with their peers, as much as consciously think out any choice they make. Equally they will 'feel' about God as much as 'think' about him.

In terms of any evangelism with children this awareness of how they make moral choices must surely affect our understanding of how they make faith choices also. From early years children do make moral choices; every parent soon becomes aware of the two or three year old wilfully disobeying rather than simply testing the parental boundaries. But they make these choices from within their limited experience and 'world view'. They will therefore generally be simple choices made without any necessary awareness of the wider implications of that choice. As the child becomes older they will have a growing awareness of how such choices affect not only themselves but others immediately around them. Then in early adolescence they will have an increasing awareness of the effects of their actions on a wider society and world. In terms of 'deciding to become a friend of Jesus', therefore, a three year old may well see little difference between that and being a friend of their mother, father or a person next door. But just because this is the case we should never ever treat that child's faith confession as unreal, unimportant or less significant than an adult's faith confession. The three year old is giving all of themselves that they know to all of Jesus that they know. We will want them, as they grow, to mature in their understanding, but we must be seeking to help that child grow within faith rather than outside it. But this leads us into our next section.

HOW CHILDREN BELIEVE

In the last ten years or so the work of James Fowler and John Westerhoff III on faith development has gained a degree of acceptance. Their concern has not simply been the development of faith in children, but the development of faith throughout our whole lifespan. Fowler's work has involved a great deal of careful research and become the subject of much debate. Westerhoff's ideas are easier to grasp and more vivid in their descriptions; they are at heart, though, largely a popularisation and interpretation of Fowler's and are not based on anything like the same degree of thorough research. Yet because of their vividness and the way in which they have rung bells in people's own experience time after time they have probably become the more popular expression of faith development ideas, at least in the UK.

In essence what both men's work and ideas have suggested is that in the earliest years of life it is the child's *experience* of faith which is most crucial to the development of their own faith. The emphasis is therefore far less on any intellectual content of 'what we must teach' and much more on children experiencing being loved, finding security in people that they can trust, and realising that the feelings of wonder and awe that every child has are real and important. Such experience will in turn develop the capacity to love, trust, hope and worship; capacities which are far more crucial to growing in faith than simply being able to regurgitate the facts about a particular Bible story. This experience will be gained primarily in the home, but can certainly be further developed through the experience of the wider community of faith in prayer, worship and being together as 'family'. It does not mean that toddlers and small children will not be told some of the very basic stories of the scriptures; they should be. But it does mean that such stories will be told within the wider framework of learning experience thus enabling children to begin to experience faith in Jesus Christ.

On reaching the age of possibly as young as six or as old as eight or nine, then whilst experience remains vital to the child's growing in faith so, increasingly, does the aspect of *joining* a faith group. It will be important for children to feel that they belong to a group, or community, of others who believe in Jesus. It may be that their own family is enough of a group, but normally it will need to be a larger group than that. A peer group will be crucial for many; the child needs to know that they belong with others like them, sharing faith in Jesus in the same way together. Ideally, though, it will not simply be a peer group. The child will really want to know that they belong to the group of all ages who are 'friends of Jesus' or 'God's family'. Hence the popularity and importance of the club and wider church community during these years. There will continue to be clear teaching of the stories of faith and a growing freedom within which the child can discover more of Jesus for themselves, but this will be based still in experiencing faith at work as part of the faith community.

Any child coming to hear of Jesus from a context in which they have previously not heard of Jesus or experienced the Christian faith at work will inevitably need a great deal of help. They will be caught in a conflict of faith experience and often be affiliated to two different faith groups, that of the Christian community and that of their own family. To have any real hope of discipling them further into the Christian faith it will be essential to try and work with the child in both faith contexts and help their parent(s) understand all that is happening with their child. We may often have to help parents gain the tools they will need to help their child grow into their own faith in Jesus. Ideally this will mean seeing the parents commit themselves to Christ as well, but if not we must do all we can to help them support their child in his or her faith in Jesus.

The next stage in the development of faith is when children start asking questions of their experience, and the experience of others. They will also ask questions of their group and the stories of faith that they have heard and accepted. Generally this *searching* begins with adolescence, but for some it may begin a little earlier, whilst for others it may be delayed into adulthood or even never arise. In this period of asking questions one would expect someone who has, for example, happily accepted the resurrection as a real fact to start asking whether or not it did really happen after all. Where the authority of the parents and heroes has been accepted it is now questioned. It can be painful for all concerned, but for real growth in faith such questioning is vital; it should never be discouraged or treated patronisingly. Asking questions is a key means of growth (remember Deuteronomy 6:20?). What will be important throughout any such searching period is that there is a safe place of belonging in which the questions can be asked without fear of rejection by the group the child has joined. Ultimately, through this searching, an individual will arrive at a new, deeper, worked-out faith which they own as their own. 'I believe it for myself' will be a key phrase at this point, alongside fresh experience, a commitment to the faith community and ongoing searching. Such an *'owned' faith* tends only to happen from early adulthood onwards. These stages of faith

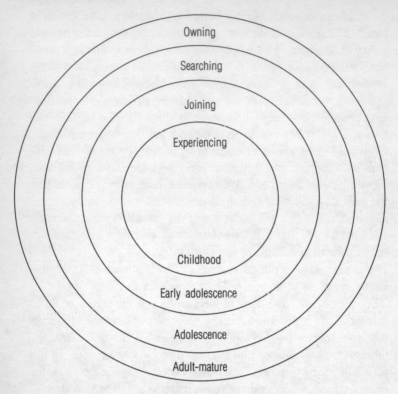

Diagram 2 – Stages of faith development

development are illustrated in Diagram 2 (following J Westerhoff's work in *Bringing up Children in Christian Faith*, Winston, 1980).

What many have failed to grasp about both Fowler's and Westerhoff's work is that they are saying that for children this faith derived from experience or 'belonging to a group' is real faith just as much as the searching and owned faith are real for the adolescent and adult. They are not even faith of a lesser order but they are of a different type. To use words like 'experienced', 'belonging' and 'searching' faith is to describe how faith is expressed at different stages of life rather than to say one is better than another.

We need to add one further point here. In one sense every child has faith. This is because faith is one aspect of being human; it is a human universal. This has been argued most helpfully by Francis Bridger in his excellent book *Children Finding Faith*. In creating us God has made trust and faith integral to being human. The Holy Spirit, as Creator Spirit, in this sense gives faith to all people. What the New Testament describes as important is *where* we place our trust. It is faith *in Christ* through which God's gift of salvation is mediated. Talk of human faith development in particular terms at different stages of life is, in the last analysis, saying nothing about the validity of that faith. The validity of any particular faith is another question.

If this distinction between faith process and faith object is accepted then there are no problems in using the insights of the faith development theorists to help us understand how children's faith may come about and be developed further, so long as we take care to treat such theories and provisional models in the same way that we use other theories of child development. If Experience and Joining are the key ways faith is both learnt and expressed in childhood then any evangelism among children will need to focus on helping children experience Jesus in a setting, or several settings, in which others who share faith in Jesus are also involved and experiencing God for themselves. Hence prayer will be crucial. So will hearing and sharing testimonies of God at work in people's lives. For some children it is *experiencing* people at worship that has a real impact. But above all it will be the experience of seeing how following Jesus affects people's lives that will be crucial. The impact on people's values and attitudes will almost certainly be the most powerful influence. In other words the Christian faith will need to be modelled to children so that they can see it is real experience affecting every aspect of Christians' lives.

It will be important that the child also experiences being part of the faith community. In the case of a child from a Christian home then this should be the faith community in the home and in the local church fellowship. If a child comes from a home where Jesus is not named as Lord and Christ then it will be the experience of the local faith community or the faith in other homes that will be invaluable. They will need to see and experience the power of the Good News expressed through the Christian community to know that it is worth joining with Jesus and his followers. The Christian community, however small, will be a powerful evangelistic tool.

As children grow they will need to be given ways and means whereby they can express their own faith in Jesus by joining a group of those who share the same faith. This may be through a club, small home group, baptism, confirmation, participation in communion, or some other way. But such expressions of faith will be real and we must treat them as seriously as those of any adults. Children who express their faith in this way should always then be treated as being in faith rather than out of it: treated as those who belong not as those on the outside.

At the heart of this coming to and growing in faith through experience and joining will be good relationships. For a child to have good experiences of faith and to have a faith group that they want to join for themselves they will need very good relationships and friendships with others of their own age and adults of faith as well. It will be very rare indeed for a child, or adult for that matter, to come to faith in Jesus outside the context of good relationships which express a concern for the total well-being of that individual. Where 'hit and run' evangelistic methods are used, any apparent response is likely to disappear rapidly unless someone comes quickly alongside and builds a good supportive, nurturing relationship.

CONCLUSIONS

When we put all of this together I believe we come to some clear guidelines about children's evangelism.

1 We should take very serious note of the age and abilities of the children with whom we work. We must present the truth of God's love in a vibrant way which is 'accessible' to those children. This will certainly mean sharing the stories of scripture, though there may be some specific stories which we feel should not be told to particularly young children (eg Jael and Sisera). We should major on God's deep love for the children, especially as revealed in Jesus.
2 We need to allow children to discover the stories and reality for themselves through active learning methods rather than merely 'telling' them.

3 We need to encourage them to experience God for themselves through prayer, worship and everyday life experiences.

4 We should happily endorse children's real responses to Jesus believing that they are perfectly capable of making such responses, whilst at the same time realising that they are responding as a five year old, ten year old or whatever.

5 We must take great care to nurture children in faith, rather than treat them as outside faith, as early on as we can.

6 We need to see good healthy relationships as central to our 'methodology'.

Some may want to ask whether or not this really is 'evangelism'. Is is not 'nurture'? Personally I want to continue to hold onto the use of the word 'evangelism' because of the way it speaks of both being and sharing Good News. I believe that what has been outlined in the last two chapters is all about God's people together and individually being the vehicle through which the Good News of God's love in Christ is made known. But in the sense that it seeks to treat children as positively as possible from their earliest days and so far as possible help them to grow 'into' and 'in' faith in Christ it is heavily dependent on a nurturing model. Perhaps we should combine the two and define children's evangelism therefore as 'nurturing evangelism' or 'evangelistic nurture'. But perhaps we have too many technical terms floating around already!

| ACTIVITIES |

1 Consider one of the sections which draws on the insights of psychology (eg 'How Children Choose'). What implications might you draw from this for your own work with children?

2 What sort of responses to Jesus do you think are appropriate for children, say, at age three, age seven and age eleven?

3 Using the learning cycle, Diagram 1, consider this chapter as an experience. What reflection, understanding and new action do you now want to make?

4 Use the tree ring diagram (p 58) to reflect on your own growth in faith.

5 How happy would you be with a term like nurturing evangelism or evangelistic nurture?

| FURTHER READING |

Children Finding Faith, Francis Bridger, Scripture Union, 1988

How Faith Grows, General Synod Board of Education, National Society/Church House Publishing, 1991

The Spiritual Life of Children, Robert Coles, HarperCollins, 1992

Children and God, Ron Buckland, Scripture Union, 1988

CHAPTER
SIX

THE GOOD NEWS FOR CHILDREN

'But what do we teach them, Paul?' is a question I am sometimes asked after trying very hard to communicate that it is relationships, and the values and attitudes that are learned through relationship, that are crucial to all our work with children and their families. It is a question I fully understand. When confronted with an epilogue at a club, or what to do in the teaching slots at a camp, we need some clear ideas about the content of the gospel.

This chapter will seek to offer at least some outlines of an answer. In particular we will consider the very basics of the Good News that we want to communicate. This is very different from a full-scale teaching syllabus that might last a Sunday group over a number of years. It tries to think of children who know nothing, or almost nothing, about Jesus; what do we want them to hear and learn?

THE FIRST YEAR

When babies first arrive in the world what they need most is to be loved and cared for. They need feeding, clothing, warmth; to feel loved and wanted. The experience of having very basic needs met; being held; knowing that someone is there and cares, will allow the baby to develop a growing feeling of being secure and wanted, and he or she will begin to develop the basics of love and trust and a sense that it is good to be alive.

This is all *feelings* gained from the values and attitudes of the parent(s) and other adults shown towards the baby. Without them the baby will begin to develop insecurity, fears, and feelings of not being sure about themselves or their own little world. This feeling of basic trust forms the root for all future development of being able to love and trust others, and accept being loved and trusted by others. There is no intellectual or cognitive element to it.

The importance of this life-stage for evangelism is profound. It means that the Christian community needs to do all it can to help parents care as fully as they are able for their child. Parentcraft classes, parent and baby groups, support through babysitting etc and welcoming parent and child in any way we can will all be crucial. This is because as we are helping the child to experience love and trust, and as we are helping them feel they are of value and importance, so we are laying the foundations for them to receive the Good News that God their Maker values and loves them very highly indeed. As we sow the seeds that will enable them to trust adults, for them the highest of beings, so we are sowing the seeds also for them to be able to grow to trust in the highest one of all, who is their loving heavenly Father (Parent).

TODDLING FORWARD

As the baby grows into a toddler they are obviously developing an ever increasing awareness of themselves and the world around them. Everything has to be tested; hence everything goes in the mouth to see what taste sensation it creates. Everything is touched to see how it feels and if it can be made to make a noise. All is glorious exploration.

Alongside this exploration, language is beginning to form; from playing with sounds, words develop. It becomes increasingly apparent to the toddler that these 'words' can be used to communicate with others and so more and more are learnt and played with so that just what each sound 'means' becomes increasingly clear. All of this leads to a growing awareness that everything is not merely an extension of themselves. Other people, and objects, come to have a life of their own. The self is slowly being differentiated from the rest of the world. It remains absolutely crucial that these enormous changes happen in a context of the child feeling loved and wanted; they need to know trust and security for them to be able to handle everything in ways which will encourage healthy growth and development. Feelings, again, rather than intellect, play the most crucial role.

The Christian community's key role must be with the child in the context of their family. It will continue to be about support through personal friendships and suitable groups such as parent support groups, parent and toddlers, pram services and the like. Prayer for and with the child will be important as it was before.

But there will be some place now for laying other foundations. The toddler is increasingly likely to enjoy stories, especially those about other toddlers. They will enjoy the Christmas story and they may enjoy other Bible stories involving babies. Care will need to be taken here: how would three year olds feel about Samuel being 'given away' at around their own age? It may well cause fear that they too will be 'given away'. So we may well choose not to tell that part of the story at this stage.

The importance of the stories during this period is not that the toddler will understand great spiritual truths but that they are being given stories that they enjoy (one criteria for deciding which ones to use) and a beginning of a language framework in which God and Jesus feature. The role of language in the developing child's ability to make sense of the world and themselves is very great. Without 'God language' being part of their formation at this stage there will be a great deal of catching up to do in later years. This means that great care needs to be taken in what language we do use about God, Jesus and the world. If our language conveys primarily ideas and feelings that make God seem very remote and unfriendly then this is clearly unhelpful. We need to ensure our God language is highly positive. We should major on God's love and greatness; his reality and faithfulness; not on his sternness and judgment. This will then act as a further criteria for our choice of biblical materials; we can use the stories that convey God's love and what a wonderful person Jesus was when he lived on the earth, particularly in the way he behaved and treated people.

Since at this age too the toddler is exploring the world and often filled with wonder and amazement at all around, we should seek to encourage this exploration and discovery of the wonders of God's world. We can use their creativity and explore experiences of water,

light, food, our bodies etc, to build further foundations for
discovering their own true selves and their Maker.

There will also be an important role in helping toddlers develop
a sense of right and wrong. At this stage parental word is absolute
law so care needs to be taken to ensure the toddler develops good
experiences of right and wrong. In this way the foundation for
understanding the need to say sorry and experience forgiveness is
also clearly laid.

It should be no great surprise if a child who is hearing about Jesus
at this age declares their love for him or their desire to be his friend.
As we have said before, any such declaration should be treated totally
positively whilst being clearly understood as the declaration of that
child at that age and that all kinds of changes to that faith are inevitable
in the years that follow. But at this stage it is a real expression of
faith.

PRE-SCHOOL

The last year or two before entering school continue to see very rapid
developments in children. The process of discovering themselves
and the world continues apace. Although the world continues to
centre around the child, the ability to distance themselves from
others and things becomes greater. Whilst still very limited, the
beginnings of being able to see things from the perspective of
someone else are now in place. Language development continues to
be crucial, as does the increasing ability to be able to control the
body and make it do more and more complex things (eg the growing
ability to kick a ball, direct it and control it).

The values and attitudes that children experience in their own
home are still absolutely crucial, but they will also be growing in
their awareness of differences in attitudes shown to them by other
adults. Hence it is vitally important that any child encountering
Christian believers picks up the values and attitudes of the rule of
God from them. The fruit of the Spirit can act as a wonderful guide
for us here alongside a real commitment to justice and God's peace.

We will still want to ensure that our God language and the Bible
stories we use share the love of God, the wonderfulness of Jesus,

the greatness of God's world and the specialness of being human (so here we may include stories of great Bible heroes *and* heroines like Abraham, David, Ruth and Mary). Special times and events will also be important, so we should make the most of the Christian festivals and experiences in the child's own life (eg birthdays, the birth of a baby brother or sister). As the awareness of right and wrong continues to grow we also continue to build an awareness of the need to say sorry and experience forgiveness. One crucial part of this learning is the willingness of adults to admit their own mistakes and say sorry to the child when that is appropriate. Parents, and other adults, do make mistakes with their children; it can only help the child develop if these mistakes are owned up to in appropriate ways.

In practical terms for churches the role of playgroups, parent support groups and other learning groups for the children themselves will be important.

SCHOOL – THE EARLY YEARS

From five to seven years the final period of laying the foundations for all future learning takes place. By the time a child is seven they have learnt somewhere around 80% of all they will ever learn; all the basic building blocks for future development in every area of life have been learnt. Even if in later life a major change occurs, such as conversion to Christ from a totally non-church background, the person will still function from this basic background; healing and change of all kinds may happen but the roots will remain fixed.

In terms of spiritual development it means that the church must continue to work as much as possible with these children and their families. The home remains the most crucial influence, although clearly changes are beginning to take place in the strength of influence held by others. The school takes a strong role; so do the child's peers, increasingly so through these years; greater note will be taken of the views of other adults and the mass media.

Our Good News must continue to be communicated primarily through relationships that convey the attitudes and values of God's rule. We should continue to emphasise the love and power of God; the specialness of Jesus; the specialness of being human; and a growing inclusion of material that highlights our responsibilities as well as our privileges. We should also continue to highlight Jesus by what he said and did, and at this stage many will be able to make at least the first steps in understanding why this good man died. In particular, many children grasp the idea of someone being punished for something someone else has done wrong, because this is quite common in their experience. The theological depths of this will be beyond them (it is in one sense beyond all of us), but the reality may be understood. The other realities of the cross, like the defeat of evil powers and the defeat of death may not be so easily grasped at this stage.

When dealing with miracles we need to be aware that because of the fantasy world of the child, and the fascination with 'magic', these may well be seen as 'magic' acts. There is inevitably a confusion between reality and fantasy which we have to help the child unravel in the years which follow this stage. Care therefore needs to be taken in how we present a miracle story if we wish to make it clear that it really happened and that it was not simply magic. Do not be surprised if they are still interpreted in a 'magic' way; what we have done by telling it otherwise is give the tools to help unravel the fact and the fiction in the following years.

The stories of great heroes and heroines will continue to be of great value as will some stories illustrating the reality of God today. We must avoid presenting Jesus as if he is locked up in the past; even the resurrection can appear to be simply a past event for these children unless we explain that he is still alive today.

At all times we should present the Bible in interesting ways, making it as 'user friendly' as possible (eg through using copies of just the text concerned rather than the whole big book) and being aware of the severe reading limitations of most at the outset of this age and many at its close. We also need to take care to present Bible stories in an imaginative yet truthful way. We must seek to handle the scriptures correctly at all times.

In practical terms we need to keep a strong emphasis on family work but there increasingly becomes a place for groups of children on their own, with parents being informed of what is happening in such groups. Any contact with the children at school is also of real value. Parents will still find immense value in well run parentcraft and parent support groups.

THE 'JUNIOR' AGE

As children move into being eight, nine, ten and eleven their mental capacities are developing further. They can place themselves in other people's positions increasingly and they grow in their own sense of independence. The heart of the gospel remains Jesus and him crucified, buried and risen again (1 Corinthians 15:3–7) and that in these actual historical events God was reconciling the world to himself (2 Corinthians 5:18ff). Hence our basic message must continue to be that of God our Maker loving each of us so deeply that he acted for us in the person of Jesus. Children at this stage are much more able to order events historically and to distinguish fact and fantasy. We must present the message as real events whose impact is still real today. Increasingly they will be able to handle the idea that Jesus is alive yet unseen, and increasingly they will be able to understand that the Holy Spirit is real and can live within us.

Heroes and heroines will also continue to be important to this age group. Yet although the 'content' of the Good News is important it remains true that the child's experience and ability to join with others will be as crucial as the intellectual content of the message. Somehow the stories must be seen to fit with the experience and life of the individual child and the group. A degree of musing and questioning will take place in every child but at this stage they will still tend to be satisfied with the answers of their authority figures (usually parents) and the convictions of their group. They will be able to understand the reality of doing things wrong against others and God, and the consequent need for forgiveness. The key understanding of the cross will still be that Jesus died 'for us', but an ever increasing grasp of his defeat of death and evil forces could come through. This is particularly so when either or both of these issues become real to the child themselves, as they do through the death of pets, grandparents, friends, a parent and the increasing involvement with occult activities by children.

Family work remains a high priority but the place of peer groups such as midweek clubs or school groups becomes increasingly important. The role of the leaders too is highly significant because they act as role models for the children of following Jesus.

EARLY ADOLESCENCE

With the onset of adolescence a major new phase of life begins. Thinking patterns begin to shift away from 'concrete' patterns and slowly into more 'abstract' ones. The whole physical and emotional upheaval of these years inevitably leads to asking the questions 'Who am I?' and 'What am I here for?' in deeper, and often more specific ways than ever before. As the years go by everything in life up to this point will be questioned. All the experiences, beliefs and people will be subjected to questioning. It means that our basic presentation of the Good News must allow for space for such questioning; it must give reasons for Christian faith. 'Because the Bible says so,' will never be a satisfactory answer in these years because it will always be countered by, 'Why does the Bible say so?' and/or, 'Can we trust the Bible anyway?'

So whilst the message is the same it will need more explaining. In today's world most children can handle most of the content of the Bible in these years, though help will still need to be given with helping young people understand it.

The role of adults outside the home could be very important, though parents must go on loving, being there and being the rock of stability through the turbulent years; often a none too easy task. So the church needs to go on supporting the parents as well as working with the young people themselves through appropriate peer and learning groups.

CONCLUSIONS

The heart of the Good News is that God, who made each of us, loves us and wants us to be with him forever. He loves us so much that even though we rebel against him he has acted to restore us to his friendship and family by sending his own Son into the world to live as a human being, Jesus of Nazareth, and then as perfect human and perfect God, to take the punishment for our wrongdoing upon himself, thereby destroying all that stands between us and God. The proof that this has been achieved is Jesus' rising again from the dead.

In response to such love all we need to do is receive God's gift of forgiveness and enter into his loving rule for ever as his child and friend.

What has been outlined in this chapter is how this good news might be mediated in content terms at different stages. When dealing with children who have not had all the foundational work suggested for the earliest years then there may well be much remedial work to be done; but this will often be in terms of emotions and language rather than other intellectual content. We may well need to build trust and love where it was not built in early life, or help a young person realise that God as Parent is not like their own unloving father (or mother). We may also need to help them come to terms with language which refers to God and Jesus as real and important when previously they were just words used unthinkingly. Without doing this then the story of Jesus may have no soil in which to take root.

The content is important; but the context and language in which that content is communicated is also crucial. The seed of the word needs to fall on good soil for it to bear fruit; the seed on its own could easily be snatched away, trampled underfoot or choked by other more vigorous growing weeds (Matthew 13: 1–23).

| ACTIVITIES |

1 Consider teaching about God as Father. What impact might early childhood experiences have on how such language is understood in later life? How might we overcome difficulties that arise here?

2 Take one of the stories of Jesus performing a miracle. How might a child of three, six, ten and thirteen react to it?

3 Create an outline programme for a parent support group to last six weeks.

| **FURTHER READING** |

Under-Fives Welcome!,
Kathleen Crawford, Scripture Union,
1990

Children Finding Faith, Francis
Bridger, Scripture Union, 1988

CHAPTER SEVEN
'LET'S BE FRIENDS'

'I just cannot make friendships with children.'

I have lost count of the number of adults who have said that to me over the past twenty years. However, many of them change their tune as they realise the importance of making friends with children and then act to develop such friendships. Some have been surprised how quickly this has happened, whilst for others it has not been easy.

In every case it has been important to be honest with God and with themselves about their initial feelings and thoughts, and to explore the reasons for these. Then there is a need to be open to the Holy Spirit to do the work of transforming people more into the image of Jesus; for if Jesus was a friend to children surely we should be as well. The same Spirit who empowered Jesus can empower us to have the same attitudes as Jesus himself. This does not mean that every Christian should be a gifted children's worker any more than they should be a gifted teacher, evangelist or prophet. However, Christians can and should be seeking to have the same attitude and actions towards children as Jesus himself. The fruit of the Spirit is, among much else, a wonderful summary of how we should all treat children, and indeed other human beings generally. If children experience love, joy, peace, patience, kindness, goodness, faithfulness, gentleness and self control they will flourish and learn these qualities for themselves (Galatians 5:22f). The fruit of the Spirit is surely the mark of true friendships.

So, relying on the Holy Spirit's power, how can we go about developing healthy relationships and friendships with children?

REMEMBER WHERE YOU CAME FROM

Roald Dahl once said that the biggest problem adults have in relating to and understanding children is that they have forgotten what it was like to be children themselves. I think he was right. When did you last sit down and recall experiences from your own childhood? The memories are there but often we have buried them away deep in our subconscious and we find it hard to discover them again. To do so would be of real value in helping us to develop friendships with children today.

Of course the world of today is very different from that of our own childhood. When I grew up through the late 1950s and 1960s I had no TV until I was five or six, and then it was black and white with BBC 1 only. Computers were enormous machines accessible only to a handful of unknown scientists. Rap, Reggae, Ragga, and Heavy Metal hadn't been thought of, and Richard Dimbleby could pull an April Fool stunt about spaghetti growing on trees and fool most of the nation because pasta was an unknown culinary delight! But the experience of being a child is no different from what it was then. The world is still an exciting place to explore and discover with real joys and real fears. The world of adults is still a world of giants (to borrow from Roald Dahl again), and the child's imagination can still run riot. So the emotional inner world of the child remains the same, as do the physical realities of size and accessibility.

For many of us recalling our own childhood is simply a matter of taking the time and trouble to explore our memories using photographs, conversations with relatives, watching old newsreels and so on. But for some, and probably more than we realise, it is a harder task. For many adults childhood was not always a pleasant experience. In order to cope with this they have buried their painful memories as deeply as they can. So it is not only hard to get in touch with those memories, it is also very traumatic, as recollections of abuse, sad experiences and hurt create pain in the present. Although buried, these experiences still affect the way in which the adult now thinks and behaves. This may be why some adults have such great difficulty in befriending children; they may need to keep a distance from children and childhood to keep their own painful memories at bay.

They will rarely be conscious of thinking like this but subconsciously that is what is happening.

If this becomes apparent when someone is in the process of rediscovering their own childhood, help may be required in the form of counselling and healing. God does heal memories if we allow him to, but often the advice and support of another Christian is needed. If you are facing a situation like this yourself then do not be embarrassed about approaching your own minister or elder, or even a professional counsellor to ask for help. You are not alone and God in his love will bring new wholeness to you through the pain.

Whether the process of remembering your childhood is relatively easy or deeply painful it can be of long term value to both understanding yourself and to being a real friend to children. On its own, however, it will not be enough.

CHILDWATCHING

So suspicious have people become in Britain today, and understandably so, that if you stood at the fence of the school playground watching children play during their break you might well be reported as acting suspiciously. This is sad but it is a sign of our modern times. It makes the next step towards developing friendships with children rather harder than it was some years ago.

Watching and observing children is vitally important for helping us to understand them. Somehow we need to place ourselves in situations where, free from suspicion, we are able to watch children at work and play. The local school is an obvious place, at least for parents. To offer to help with children's reading and writing, or to help at school functions or trips, puts us in a position of being able to watch and listen to them. Likewise in local churches simply to look on at a Sunday group or a midweek club and observe the children in action can be hugely instructive. Parents probably do not spend enough time just watching and listening to their own children at play around the home to discover more of what they enjoy, are thinking and so forth. Too often parents, and teachers, spend most of their communication time with children managing them rather than listening to and relating to them. Sensitively observing children at play in the local park or on the street, or taking the occasional walk around the local toy shop, to look at the toys and listen to children make comments is quite instructive. Calling at local newsagents to buy a selection of the current popular comics and magazines, or sitting down to watch some children's TV and early evening programmes will also help us gain a further grasp of what interests them, what influences them and what are the 'in' words, pop singers and crazes. The combination of observing children in the home, at school, in the park or wherever, and observing their world of toys, gadgets, TV and magazines will build up quite a picture of what it is like to be a child today.

By careful observation of children themselves and the world they inhabit we will be able to build some kind of bridge between the world of our own childhood and the world of today's children. Our emotions as children were very similar to those of children today; it is simply the context in which those emotions are aroused and operated that has changed so drastically. It can only help us to be better informed of that context if we are to befriend children today.

DO THINGS WITH CHILDREN

Remembering our own childhood and observing children today are, I believe, very important aspects for an adult wanting to befriend a child, but they will not, in themselves, create a friendship. To do this we must actually meet and *do* things with a child.

It is a sad reflection, but probably a true one, that parents spend little time simply being with their children playing games or going out together. Time spent with a son or daughter is surely never wasted time. I meet so many parents who tell me that they simply do not know how to play with their own children. No wonder many parents and children do not feel they are each other's friends. Yet I believe that parents and children should be the best of friends.

If any adults really want to befriend children then it will be vitally important that they do things together. A friend of mine, an excellent children's worker, once told me, 'Every Sunday morning we have a Bible story and pray and so on; its good but I really feel that the best times with the children are when we go out swimming or play football in the park. Then we really seem to click, and we have really good chats about God and them.' I think he has grasped the real lesson of experience here, that it is our friendships and relationships with children which are crucial. They will play a much greater role in communicating God's love to them than any amount of Bible stories told in isolation from life. If you want to start developing a friendship with a child simply get on and do something together; climb a tree, go swimming, play a game, make a model, go for a walk; it does not matter too much what you do so long as it is wholesome, done together and with the full knowledge of his or her parents.

TALK TOGETHER

Once you start doing things together you will inevitably start talking together. Some of us are naturally chattier than others but all of us need to talk. Talk about what you are doing; find out about the child, *and let the child find out about you.*

The most expert person I know at this is David Lewis, SU evangelist of many years. One boy returning from Longbarn camp declared to his parents, 'Mr Lewis does nothing all day except whittle wood.' The parents, probing their son a little further, asked 'Does Mr Lewis do anything while he is whittling wood?' 'Oh yes,' said the boy, 'he talks to children all the time.' In fact Mr Lewis did a lot more, but the boy's observation speaks volumes. He had himself spent hours whittling wood with Mr Lewis at camp and had talked about almost everything under the sun. He will remember those conversations for the rest of his life though he will probably forget 99% of the content of the conversations themselves. The experience of talking with an adult, feeling valued and cared for because that adult listened and shared something of himself was probably the most crucial communication of God's love that he had experienced that week.

We will always need to take care with our language when talking to children (and I don't mean simply avoiding bad language!). The younger they are the more limited their vocabulary, so we need to use words they will understand. We should always avoid talking over children's heads (literally as well as figuratively) and talking down to them (again literally and figuratively). We need to talk as equals, making allowances for each other's personality and level of comprehension. But then this should be true when two adults talk together as well, shouldn't it!

FRIENDSHIPS TAKE TIME

Friendships do not just happen. Sometimes we meet someone and hit it off straight away; in a matter of days, even hours, we can feel we have known the person for years. But usually friendships take time. This is bound to be true of developing friendships with children. Children are remarkably quick at making friends as they are generally less inhibited than adults, but it still takes time.

None of us can be friends with *everyone*. Some people want to be friends with everyone, and try to be as an expression of their own need to be loved and feel secure. But in fact each of us can only cope with a limited number of friendships. I am continually impressed by the pattern that Jesus followed in the Gospels: he had a large circle of friends, but within that circle had twelve particular friends, within that a smaller group of three (Peter, James and John), and had an even more intimate friendship with one (John). If Jesus was comfortable with this then surely we should be content with a small number of very close friendships, a wider circle of friends and perhaps an even wider circle of acquaintances. In developing friendships with children, therefore, we must be content to develop only one or two really strong friendships whilst having more friends than that.

In this combination of intimate and less intimate friendships we need to avoid any sense of favouritism. Somehow in the Gospels, whilst there was clearly rivalry and jealousy between the disciples (eg Mark 9: 33ff and 10: 35ff), none of them apparently ever accused Jesus of showing favouritism to John or Peter. They must all have felt equally valued and loved by Jesus even if he apparently gave more time and attention to some than others. If this was the case then we too can live with varied levels of friendship without having favourites. Because none of us is perfect we are bound to fail in this at times. Favouritism will rear its ugly head and threaten to damage our relationships with some children. When it does we need to be aware of it as quickly as possible. (Often it will need someone else to point it out to us and this may well be the child who is feeling less favoured!) We then need to confess it to God, ask forgiveness of those we have failed and then get on with being a friend again, knowing that God has forgiven us as he forgives all our failures. Admitting that we are bound to fail sometimes is no excuse, however, for not seeking, in the power of the Spirit, to aim for the perfect standard that has been set before us by Jesus himself.

CONCLUSION

The whole of this chapter has emphasised the importance of developing friendships with children and suggested things that should help us to do this. At the end of the day, however, you can read and re-read this chapter until you are blue in the face and you will not have made any friendships with children. What we all need to do is go out and get on with it by simply being with children, doing things with them and getting to know them. But whatever activities we seek to arrange for children, at the heart of them all must be this desire to develop good friendships with them. In technical jargon this is called 'Relational Evangelism and Nurture', which means that to be really effective, evangelism and nurture of children must take place in the context of loving, caring relationships rather than in any other way. This raises major questions about the validity of any form of short term or 'hit and run' style evangelism with children. It will mean that in whatever ways we seek to share the Good News of Jesus with children and see them develop into mature believers we must be willing to pay the price of developing long-term costly friendships with them.

Part of this cost must be to develop good long term relationships with the child's family as well. If we are going to relate to children in their full social context this relating to the wider family will be vital. It is also extremely important from the parent's view that they know any adults who are having anything to do with their children.

Any responsible parent will be concerned that their children are safe in our hands.

So, make friends with children; make friends with the family.

| ACTIVITIES |

1 Either on your own or in a group do some recalling of childhood memories. It may help to do this by considering these questions.

- What events can you remember from your own childhood and how did you feel about them?
- Who were your adult friends in childhood and what role did they have in your life then?

Remember, if this raises real hurts then don't be afraid to share them with someone and bring them to God for healing.

2 Go and do some sensitive childwatching using the observation sheet provided. If at all possible discuss with others your observations so that you can compare and contrast your findings with theirs.

3 Take a visit to a local newsagents, toy shop and video shop and take a good look at what's available for children. How are these different from what was available when you were a child?

What are the exciting things (eg toys, books, videos) in the child's world that you can relate to and share with them as you develop a friendship?

4 Watch some children's TV and discuss it with both children and adults. In your discussion, focus mainly on feelings, values and anything learned. This will help you get to know each other better and so further develop relationships.

| FURTHER READING |

Yesterday's Child, Mary Pytches, Hodder & Stoughton, 1990

Children at Play, David Porter, Kingsway, 1989.

OBSERVATION SHEET

Make sure you use this sensitively and wisely. Ideally you need to observe a number of children to be able to draw comparisons across age ranges etc. Also try to compare and contrast your observations with those of others.

To make these observations, you might visit a local school, by arrangement with the headteacher; or go to your own church midweek club or Sunday activity; or you could visit someone else's home.

It is suggested that you use a separate sheet for each child. You may photocopy this sheet for this specific purpose.

1 What do you note about the child's physical size?

4 What is the child actually doing?

2 What do you observe about the child's physical coordination skills (eg do they look awkward or in full control of their limbs etc)?

5 Does any of the child's play involve the use of role play (eg pretending to be mums and dads, a TV character, or a sporting hero)? In what ways is this expressed?

3 How old do you think the child is?

6 How does the child communicate (eg by talking, physical touch, looks and glances)
   (a) with other children?
   (b) with adults?

9 If you hear the child talking, what kind of language does he or she use? (Eg are the words of one, two or more syllables; are sentences grammatical?)

7 What things does the child appear to enjoy doing and for how long? Why do you think they are enjoying this?

10 Do you pick up any clues through your observation about the child's moral values? If so, what are they?

8 What things appear to frustrate or bore the child, and why?

11 Do you pick up any clues through your observation about the child's spiritual values? If so, what are they?

FOR ALL THE FAMILY

Annie had thoroughly enjoyed her summer holiday. It was a Scripture Union camp for eight to eleven year olds. Then in October she was back again. This time on a week for the whole family. She came with her mum and baby sister. (Dad had opted out of the family.) During the week there was a mixture of events for everyone together, children on their own and adults on their own. It was a lot of fun in the midst of which the reality of God's love was shared by the team. Annie's mum came to a point of real commitment to Christ. She felt different immediately and returned home knowing that while life would not be any easier, Christ would be with her and the two children in a way they had never known before. Together they would seek to follow Christ, but they were not alone. The wider family of Christ would be there to support them as well.

So far in this book we have placed strong emphases on two points in children's evangelism. First, it must be based on relationship; and second, it should, wherever possible, be within the context of the wider family. In the last chapter we concentrated on personal relationships with children; in this one we will explore practical ways in which we can evangelise whole families (whatever their make up).

THE CHURCH AS FAMILY

The early church, it appears, did not have to go out of its way to evangelise. Instead as we read the Acts of the Apostles we find people being drawn towards the early church. The praise, activities and lifestyle of these first Christians was attractive to those outside it. As one person has put it, 'The life of the early church was an event that needed explaining.' So often today it seems that churches can easily be ignored; no explaining is ever asked for. Why is this?

Many argue strongly for a recovery of the 'power' ministry of the early church. 'We need signs and wonders,' they argue. I am sure there is a degree of validity in this. Surely we all want what the Father desires for his people, and to know as much of the power of the Holy Spirit as possible. But we ignore the warnings and words of Jesus at our peril. He said himself that resurrection would not convince some people of his reality (Luke 16:31), so what chance lesser miracles? He also had some sharp warnings for those who were interested in him only because of the miraculous things he did (John 6:25ff). But above all we would do well to ponder these words, 'By this all men will know that you are my disciples, if you love one another' (John 13:35). It seems to me that these are the words that rang through the hearts and minds of the early Christians. They knew that it was their love for God expressed through their love for one another which was of paramount importance. Why not take time yourself to read again John's first letter and 1 Corinthians 13?

This is where we need the Spirit's power in fullest measure. Every local Christian community, whatever its denominational tag or doctrinal emphasis, should be seeking to be a loving community. The image of the 'family' is one which is helpful for such a community. It implies that everyone belongs, whether married, unmarried, widowed, divorced, young, old, male, female, black, brown, white, yellow, learned, unskilled, able-bodied, or 'disabled'. Above all perhaps 'family' implies that relationships lie at the heart of being God's people.

It does not take a genius to see the connection with family evangelism. If we want to be a people concerned for whole families then we need to be seeking to be God's family ourselves. Family evangelism will come primarily from local churches being loving family communities themselves. They will then be attractive to those outside of Christ. We will be an event for which people will want an explanation. This may well mean that before we do anything else, we need to spend time working at being an all-age community of believers who really do value each other.

We need to ask questions of our regular worship. Is it marginalising children? Or young people? Or singles? What of the teaching content of our services? Do we really believe and practice that we are all fellow learners? Are children encouraged to give as well as receive? If we have separate groups for children, are the leaders ready to learn from the children, or is it all one way from the 'teacher' to the child? Do we regularly run activities when all ages can be together and enjoy each others company, learn from one another, worship God together, pray for each other, listen to God together and just have fun together?

The local community of believers should be 'home' for all ages together. A place where hurts, fears, disagreements, joys and laughs can be openly shared together. A place where gifts are recognised, encouraged and developed in every individual. Above all a place of loving acceptance and growing holiness. It will then be a community that welcomes 'the stranger' and is open to new people joining it. It will be primarily an organism rather than an organisation, living and growing rather than hemmed in and in danger of dying. It will be a people on the move, open to change, not an institution stuck in its ways.

Lest you think that this is all doomed to failure before the start because 'no local church is ever really like that', let me encourage you to think differently. In the privileged position of working for Scripture Union and therefore visiting many different churches of all denominations, sizes and social backgrounds, I have seen many churches which show signs of being this type of community. In my experience this has been enough for hundreds of non believers. They know that the local church is not perfect; they would run a mile if it was because it would offer them no hope at all. But time and again people have said something like this to me, 'When I came here I was made to feel so welcome. There was a love here I have never experienced anywhere else.' So often when we are on the inside of the church fellowship we are only aware of the problems, failures, and weaknesses of that fellowship. We lose sight of the grace of God at work in people's lives helping them through those problems. This grace is building friendships and support across social barriers; it is making Christ real to people. In the grace of God it is often this that the outsider sees and this that attracts them towards Christ. So let us seek to love one another, not so much to be good individual Christians but to be the people of God where we know our imperfections and experience the grace of God as we follow him together.

Then, alongside of this, we can arrange some specific events where Jesus can be shared, often in a very informal, low key way, to the whole family together.

FAMILY TO FAMILY

In a household where Jesus is Lord it makes sense that from time to time members of that household will want to pray together, share together and perhaps read the Bible together. Different households find different patterns for doing this. Indeed these patterns may even change as time passes. Occasionally, too, each household will want to open their home to others. So why do we not use whole household units in evangelism? *The Good News Down The Street* programme is now well established for home-based evangelism, though it seems to be used with adults only. With some adaptation it could be used for evangelising whole family groups. A family of Christians could invite a neighbouring household (which may be a family but might equally well be a single person living alone) to their home for a meal and a time of exploring together as a family. They might look at a Bible story together, use a video and then play games, do craft activities related to a theme and simply learn together more of Jesus. This could happen over a period of weeks. The learning will not all be one way; often the insights of non believers make a great impact on the believers as well as vice versa. It may also be helpful where there is a mixture of believers and non believers in the same household. The whole intention is to provide a secure atmosphere in which each is relating to the others across age, interest and faith differences, sharing their values, attitudes and thoughts, and learning from one another. It is trying to express something of the rule of God in a family or household setting.

This may be asking too much too soon. Why not simply go out to the theatre, the seaside or the park together from time to time? But do things together and naturally share Jesus in those settings over a period of months, even years. As friendships develop then all kinds of things will be shared and learned. I want to stress again it will not all be one way learning. God will surprise us and use non believers to teach us more about ourselves and himself. Of course, there will be individual chats and happenings in the midst of all this but we need to use times together far more than we do at present.

Two or three families or households may even decide to go away together for a weekend or longer, and agree to spend a little time each day exploring something about Jesus and the Bible. (In the chapter 'Taking the Kids Away' we will look more closely at residential events.) This idea is explored more fully in John Hattam's very helpful booklet, *Family Evangelism*. He calls such family groups 'Clumps'. I am convinced we would do well to explore this idea far more fully and as we do so people will come up with a host of creative ideas.

FAMILY FUN NIGHTS

These have become increasingly popular over the past few years. Sometimes they form part of the programme of a holiday club or term time week aimed mainly at children, but they can easily be organised as events in their own right almost anytime of the year.

A number of games can be played at these, all of them team games suitable for people of all ages and involving little equipment, all of which is readily available. Some examples are skittles, shove ha'penny, velcro darts, ball in bucket, tunnel ball, and polos on straws relay. Throughout the evening teams can take part in all the games. Sometimes several teams can play one game together, at others there might be a series of games going on around the room. The emphasis is on fun and doing things together.

Food and drink can be offered as part of the evening. Then, either in the middle or towards the close of the evening, it may be appropriate to bring everyone together and have a brief testimony from a church member, a very brief talk, or show a short video. It is important in any publicity that this is made clear so that people who come do not have it sprung on them as a surprise. A short, snappy presentation of the gospel to all ages in this context can be very powerful. Such an event need not be in the evening. It might be more appropriate to hold it on a Saturday or Sunday afternoon, and if the local park is available use that. (Just mind the dog's mess!)

A variant on the games evening is to involve everyone in some kind of creative activity. In *Family Evangelism* John Hattam describes a 'Family Coat of Arms' evening where each family designs and makes their own coat of arms. This encourages families to talk together about what is important to each of them and what they would want to have as symbols for their life together. Then they have to cooperate in actually producing something. It need not be a coat of arms – I have been involved in family groups creating some very fine fire engines out of supplied boxes and paints. The range of possibilities is endless. Any nuclear family unit working together on these type of evenings should be encouraged to be an extended family for the evening. Two or three family groups may join together or single people included in with the family group for that evening. It is important that so far as possible everyone is made welcome at such events.

Further variants on this type of event would include barbecues, 'Food from around the World' evenings, quiz nights, barn dances and events which involve more of a presentation.

FAMILY PRESENTATION EVENTS

Alyn Haskey has cerebral palsy. He is consequently confined to a wheelchair and has speech difficulties, but he is highly intelligent and a very gifted evangelist. He is one person with whom I have been involved at a presentation for the whole family. The evening included poetry, puppets, music, interview-style testimony and a Christian magician. Through the whole evening the gospel was shared with people of all ages.

On other occasions drama sketches, interspersed with interviews, music and food both indoors and outdoors has worked well. Perhaps even more simply a family showing of a film like *The Hiding Place*, *Tanglewoods Secret*, *Treasure of the Snow* or *Cry from the Mountain* can speak to people of all ages together. However, if you do this using video please use several small screens or hire a large image video projector.

On a larger scale Scripture Union has organised a number of Scrap Happy tours. These are plays specifically commissioned from professional Christian playwrights and performers which have toured the country playing in venues for around 500 people. The plays themselves have explored various aspects of 'family' relationships and communicated something of God's good news for all ages. Local churches should keep their eyes open for larger events like this that they can take non believers to as whole family groups and then follow it up back at home. There is no reason, however, why some larger churches, or groups of churches, should not attempt some local 'amateur' dramatic events. Non believers could be involved in the whole production process. I know quite a number of churches who put on pantos at Christmas or musical evenings, so why not put on similar events with a clear Christian content as well?

Such presentation evenings are a far cry from the evenings where children perform pieces for their parents and others to watch. No doubt children usually enjoy performing in this way, and parents like watching their children do things. It does give both a right sense of pride and achievement. I have to say, however, that I can never remember such an event leading to any response to the gospel, nor have I ever heard of anyone responding in such a setting. (That's guaranteed a few letters to correct me!) So whilst not necessarily wanting to abandon them entirely I do want to suggest that we look for more creative ways of being and doing things together along the lines of the ideas suggested above.

Over the last few years another type of presentation evening for all ages together has become popular, particularly in more 'charismatic' circles. These are often called 'Family Praise' parties. The large bulk of the evening is usually given over to lively music and singing. Everyone is encouraged to enjoy the music and dance, jump, clap and generally boogie. The songs are mainly songs of praise to God. The evening also includes some prayer (both led from the front and done in small groups around the hall) and teaching. There may be mime or drama as well. Often these events attract large numbers of mainly Christian families, but some non believers do attend. Personally I have found them hugely enjoyable and I know that many children and adults have been glad to be part of them. No doubt some, perhaps many, people have found real spiritual help through them, and may even have become Christians through them.

However, there is a need for some caution about such events. Some people (not the main leaders of such events) seem to suggest that these are *the* way to evangelise families. This is a strong overstatement of their role. The style definitely appeals to many, but it puts others off. The lack of actually getting people of all ages to talk to each other or do anything genuinely relational is a real weakness. There is a real danger of young children in particular making a purely emotional response to such a lively enjoyable event. Too often we ignore the emotional response to Christ, but if it is only emotional it will soon fizzle out and then there is the danger that for those children Christianity will be rather like day-old flat Coke, something to be avoided for the rest of their lives.

Hence if we do organise such events, we need to take great care. They are one style of event amongst a wide range. We can alter the content in places to encourage greater genuine interaction of people and take very great care in how we handle any appeals for response. A low key appeal, if any, and very thoughtful counselling will be needed.

FAMILY GATHERINGS

In a society in which all the pundits tell us the family is 'falling apart', if the church really does believe it is important to help families not only stay together but grow together, then more time must be given simply to helping families *be* together. As this happens many non believing families may join in because they also want to work at being together. Many churches have tried a variety of ways of making time for families to be together, such as hiring a local swimming pool one evening a week or every fortnight and inviting church members to come and bring their neighbours; using church halls for badminton evenings, or hiring the local sports centre for the same purpose; organising and running family workshops where around the venue a variety of activities can take place – for example, sewing, bicycle maintenance, board games or keep fit with an area for serving drinks and where people can chat. People of all ages should be in each group – couples, singles, or families. Sometimes families can do things together, or they can split up around the groups. The evening is rounded off with everyone together for perhaps a sing-song, parachute games, or a story. Whilst there people can get to know each other and talk about their lives. Christians and non Christians work and play alongside each other and, in time, some people may move from being outside Christ to in Christ. They would never have dreamed of going to a Sunday service before this.

Through it all the church community is seeking to be a living community of faith which serves the community in which it is set. The church is to be the community for *others*, not the community for itself.

GOD'S FAMILY IN THE COMMUNITY

Too many churches seem to exist for their own sake rather than for the glory of God and the service of others. Each local church, or group of local churches, should really be seeking to serve their local community as fully as possible. In this way we will be God's light in our locality, and people are drawn towards this light just as they were drawn towards Jesus himself. Therefore we need to find ways in which we can serve our local community. The possibilities are almost endless. We should be involved in caring for individuals in their particular need, whether it be the lonely housebound person or the refugee fearing deportation. We should be concerned about the environment of the area; the provisions for safe play areas, traffic schemes, tree planting etc. We should seek justice for everyone in the neighbourhood. We can pray for our neighbours and for the area, and we can tell the Good News of Jesus. This is showing concern for the total well-being of all the people in our area, concerned for the well-being of every child whether or not they ever enter our buildings. It is about being and sharing the Good News with children where they are rather than expecting them to come to us before we share God's love with them.

In this context there are a number of other ways of working with the whole family.

1 PLAYGROUPS

A local church playgroup can be a terrific resource for families with pre-school children. When well organised and run they provide a safe place for children to play, and therefore to discover and learn. They help young children develop their social skills as they meet and play with a range of other children. For parents they also offer friendly support and advice with the leaders and other parents. I have personally known of a number of parents whose first contact with the church community has been through a playgroup. Through the relationships that have subsequently developed they have come to find Christ for themselves. This means, of course, that the child is now being raised in a home where Christ is Lord, which in turn must be of great benefit to their own discovery of Jesus.

2 PARENT AND TODDLER GROUPS

A similar function is often played by parent and toddler groups. Here there is an additional advantage that the parents are usually present throughout the session, thus giving more time for good relationship building. To be really effective these groups need to be seen as real opportunities to help parents and children relate together as they play and do things together. Thankfully there is a growing body of material available to help the organisers of these groups arrange such activities. The groups also need to be seen as times of building up relationships between adults. If alongside this there can be sensitive visiting of homes, the long term impact can be very profound.

Contact through parent and toddler groups and playgroups or nurseries sometimes arises when parents enquire about having their child 'christened' or 'blessed'. It is not the purpose of this book to argue the pros and cons of infant baptism or dedication. However, there does need to be an openness of spirit towards a parent making any kind of approach towards a church regarding 'having their child done'. The very act of approach shows some glimmer of interest and concern about God; it may arise from all kinds of superstitious ideas but it is real. Therefore we need to be as positive as we can be towards parent and child alike. How each church will actually work this out in practise is up to them, but to give a wholly negative response towards such an approach could well be permanently damaging in terms of relationships with the parent. This in turn will be passed on to the child and may contribute towards them developing a negative attitude towards Jesus. A positive response is no guarantee of seeing conversion at a later date but it must help. Any opportunity is a God-given one and should be welcomed with open arms knowing that God's Spirit is always at work, drawing people to Jesus.

3 PARENTCRAFT

Parents are given very little preparation or help for their lifelong task of being parents. You can have a child quite freely without any training or qualifications, yet it is arguably the most responsible task a person will ever have. Inevitably everyone tends to model their own parenting on the way they were parented. Either they are happy with the way they were raised and follow the same pattern, or they deliberately change their own policy because they felt hard done by. Many parents feel this is a real strain. Every single church should consider running courses in parentcraft and open them up to the whole community. This does not mean simply arranging to show a series of James Dobson videos! These contain some material that is helpful but they are not the total answer, and some assertions made in them are not quite so certain as the presentation suggests.

The real value in parentcraft sessions is in bringing parents together to talk openly about the issues of concern to them. They can be run in a context of loving honesty, mutual listening and respect, and based again on developing relationships where these things can grow. Learning is through sharing experience, reflecting on it, reaching some ideas through this process, and going away to put them into action which in turn may lead to further reflection. In other words the learning cycle will be in operation and through it parents will learn to parent in a way which more closely reflects the rule of God in their own lives and the life of their household. If the Christian community is helping parents to be better parents it must consequently be helping the children experience greater well-being under the rule of God. This has to be good news for everyone concerned, for making Jesus known to children and families.

CONCLUSIONS

Family evangelism needs to be high on our agendas. All the ideas in this book for events specifically designed for children should be planned in tandem with all-age events. This is not an either/or choice but a both/and strategy. The various suggestions made in this chapter have been tried and tested in a wide variety of settings by all sorts of people, but they are only a beginning. Every church should seek to be as creative as possible, coming up with new ideas or variations of old ones which will be appropriate for their own particular setting. However, this should not be mainly a question of events and ideas but a question of attitude and lifestyle. The church is called to be 'family'. If we have not got this clear then all the methods and programmes in the world will be ineffective. God as Father, Son and Spirit is 'family'; we are called to reflect this in our life as God's community within the local community in which we are set. As we do so we will find ourselves reaching out to whole family units, whatever their make up may be.

| ACTIVITIES |

1 Consider your own church fellowship. How much is it seeking to be 'God's family'? You may find it useful to consider some of the questions in the section 'The Church as God's Family'.

A very useful resource for exploring this fully is the Scripture Union DIY Training Pack, 'Making Time For The Family'.

2 Arrange an afternoon or evening for families to do something together (eg swimming or decorating the church hall).

3 Prayerfully consider ways in which your church could start or further develop family evangelism.

| **FURTHER READING** |

Family Ministry, Joe Leonard, Scripture Union, 1988

Family Evangelism, John Hattam, Scripture Union Missions Department, 1989

Splash, Christine Orme and Christine Wood, Scripture Union, 1992

Under Fives Welcome, Kathleen Crawford, Scripture Union, 1990

Parents and Under Fives, Judith Wigley, Marshalls, 1990

How to Really Love Your Child, Ross Campbell, Scripture Press, 1987

Good News Down The Street, Michael Wooderson, Grove Books, 1982

Seen and Heard, ed. David Merritt, JBCE/Scripture Union Australia, 1986

What Will We Do With The Children? David Merritt and Muriel Porter, JBCE, 1990

CLUBS, GROUPS AND THEIR LIKE

Family evangelism is a must if we are to reach children effectively with the gospel, but we will often still find ourselves working with children in peer group situations. Whilst these should always be placed within a wider strategy their role will be crucial for many. Such peer groups take many different forms and are called all kinds of wonderful things, such as Crunchies, 7211, Chattabox and J Team. Here we will look at some of them.

SUNDAY SCHOOLS AND THEIR LIKE

Personally I do not like the name Sunday School. It sounds too formal and too like what happens from Monday to Friday. As the Church of England report, *Children In The Way*, points out, historically Sunday Schools have largely operated on a 'school' model, with classes, teachers, pupils and lessons all being part of the language. This model has many weaknesses, the chief of which is that it tends to treat children as recipients and never as givers. We have already argued strongly for the use of the 'family' model in relation to church life. Whilst accepting that this too has limits, it was too quickly dismissed in *Children In The Way*. That particular report went almost single mindedly for the 'pilgrim' model for the church which sees the whole Christian community as being on a journey together. Each individual has their own 'faith journey' but they journey together with others. This certainly has great strengths. It is biblical, allows us to see everyone as equal pilgrims, and allows children to help adults, even to lead them at times rather than the other way around. However, to plump solely for one model, as happened with the 'school' one, is to run the risk of missing out on truths that a different model highlights. If anything we need to retain the good aspects of all three models, 'pilgrim', 'family' and 'school', whilst remaining aware of the deficiencies of each. To be fair, many Sunday Schools have changed their style, name and methods for quite a number of years now. Some of the well used published materials do actually operate on a 'pilgrim' or 'family' model (eg Scripture Union's Learning Together materials), or even a combination of all three. For the purposes of this book, however, there is a deeper problem. 85% of children do not go near Sunday Schools, however radically they have changed their names, styles or methods. The large bulk of the 15% who do attend these groups are the children of believing families or families on the fringe of church life. The downward trend of Sunday School attendance since 1945 has been well documented in the opening chapter of *All God's Children?*

The pattern of life in Britain has changed radically. Sunday is now a major leisure day. An increasing number of major sporting events are held on Sunday; many amateur leagues play their games on Sundays, and swimming baths are often crowded out. In the summer months the countryside and beaches are crowded out on Sundays. Increasingly Sunday is also a day for shopping. No longer is Sunday School the only option to a boring morning at home. By and large bed, TV, videos or leisure activities fill the day for children. More and more parents are not sending their children to church on Sundays but instead allow the children to 'choose for themselves' or may even discourage them from church. In order to reach the 85% of children who do not come, churches need to do some radical rethinking about Sunday groups and the rest of the week.

MIDWEEK CLUBS

Many churches have been running midweek clubs for a long while. In many places there is still an insistence that attendance at the midweek club is conditional on attendance on a Sunday. I understand the thinking behind this but it is fundamentally flawed. First, it fails to acknowledge the realities of life today. The changed nature of

Sundays and of attitudes to church means that such a rule will generally tell against the non-churched child. But it also is theologically shaky. It creates an impression of Christianity being about law rather than grace. It establishes a system of reward which does not accord with the gospel: 'If you keep the Sabbath then you will be rewarded with the midweek club.' Further it fails to establish friendship-based evangelism as central to its thinking. Wherever I come across this pattern there is either an explicit statement or implicit idea that 'we teach them on Sunday and they can have their "fun" midweek.' If the best way to share Christ with children is to befriend them, be with them and allow them to see and hear of Christ through our own lives, then the fundamental place for them to discover Christ is the club night rather than the Sunday group.

Some will accuse me of stereotyping this situation. 'Our Sunday groups are more active and fun than that,' they will say. I am quite prepared to accept that they are. Nevertheless, there is almost always a difference in ethos and feel between the two events, and club will usually win out in the children's eyes. I am not suggesting that the Sunday group should be abandoned, but it may need changing. The midweek club could be made far more open to the non-churched child because he or she may be freer to attend midweek than on Sundays.

So how should midweek clubs be run? At the heart of them there needs to be a real love for the children amongst the leaders and a desire to befriend them, care for them and so to share Christ with them. This should be at the root of any of the organised activities. From there on variety is the spice of life. Some clubs might be geared around very specific interests and activities; for example, many churches are running successful children's drama and dance groups or sports teams. Others concentrate on crafts, like clay modelling, art, woodwork and cookery. The most common club, however, would be more general in nature, a mixture of quiet and noisy games, occasional craft activities, music, drinks and chats. By the end of the session the leaders will have got to know the children who are there and, over a period of weeks, months, even years, they can develop friendships with and share Jesus with them. The leaders can also develop friendships with parents as they bring or collect their children, through holding occasional family nights, by saying hello and chatting at the school gate or in the shops, or through visiting their homes.

In many clubs there is a short epilogue, often in the middle of the session, when something about Christ is shared specifically. This may be a talk, but hopefully more often it will be through drama, video, story, game, discussion or a combination of these. There is always a danger that the 'God slot' will be the boring bit of the club. Make sure it is not! With thought and effort many clubs should be able to create a fully integrated programme so that the 'God slot' is not an isolated event. Crafts, games and activities could all be geared toward helping the children explore a particular point about God and his ways. Suppose, for example, you wanted to communicate something about Jesus as the Bread of Life (not the easiest of concepts for many children to grasp). You could do some bread making; have a bread tasting session with all sorts of bread available (pitta, nan, granary, wholemeal, or soda); play games involving flour and water (the messier the better); read part of John 6; create a drama; or if a Christian baker is available get him or her to come along. The whole event could be excellent fun and would help children understand Jesus far better than through a five minute talk, even if it is illustrated and told brilliantly. Ideally, such an integrated programme would be the normal standard week by week. If, however, this seems too demanding, to run one from time to time as part of the clubs variety would be excellent.

In all club activities care needs to be taken to ensure that everyone is catered for appropriately. This may mean a number of activities going on at the same time. You may need a quiet corner for draughts, chess or Connect 4, perhaps a computer corner, areas for table tennis, table football, pool, or snooker, and an area for buying food and drink. Crafts might be going on in another area or a separate room. What you do depends partially on the facilities available, but it is surprising how much you can pack into a fairly small space.

In all of these activities the role of the leaders is crucial. They need to be well prepared, in control and ready to cope with the unexpected. The most important thing, however, is to be there consistently. A good stable leadership is vital for the building up of good relationships both with the children and their parents. This means a good ratio of leaders to children; if there are too few leaders then their role becomes that simply of managers or policemen, and good relationships cannot be built (see Chapter 14 on Leadership). Clubs can be run for a range of ages. Children at any stage of primary school and early secondary school enjoy being part of a club. Care must be taken as to how wide an age range is included and to ensure that the activities provided are suitable for the ages and abilities of the children who come. (Typically you may run a club for groups aged 5–7+, 8–10+ and 11–13+). The timing of such clubs can also vary. They may be after school or in the early evening; on any day of the school week; or it may be that a Saturday morning, afternoon or evening, or perhaps even a Sunday evening would be the most suitable time. Such decisions need to be made locally on the basis of when most children are likely to be available and adequate leadership can be provided.

WORKING IN SMALLER GROUPS

Small group activities ought to be part of the staple diet of children's activities. Even in a club of forty or fifty children there should be times and places where the children are operating in much smaller groups of maybe three or four, perhaps seven or eight. This will happen naturally in a format where several activities are taking place at once. Two playing pool whilst two more watch; five or six doing a craft activity together; two playing Connect 4 as one looks on, and so on. Leaders can be scattered around, joining in the activities and generally ensuring that every child is happy. At times when larger groups are operating together it would be invaluable to break down into smaller groups for discussion, activity, prayer or whatever. Then leaders could be scattered amongst these smaller groups. They need not actually lead the group – it is good for children to be given this responsibility sometimes – but they can join in the group's activities. Once again consistency of leadership will help build good relationships and enable the groups to function well.

The reason for using smaller groups should be obvious. It is impossible to develop relationships of any depth in large groups; the small group is the place where children will be able to get to know each other and get to know the adults. Such groups should become places of openness and security. Very often children will take the lead in opening up about their lives though some are always rather more reticent. The adult's role is to be one of the group whilst continuing to exercise responsibility.

In some settings, however, small groups can exist purely in their own right rather than as a small part of a larger activity. We will now turn to these.

In some settings club leaders reach a point where they feel that they are little more than policemen/women in the club. The children have needed so much watching and correcting that there has been little time for building meaningful relationships. This often arises in situations where the ratio of leaders to children has been inadequate, or where the premises have had so many nooks and crannies that all sorts of things go on out of sight. Sometimes even with the best of premises and good ratios this has still happened. Rather than just go on like this they may decide to abandon the club-style entirely and concentrate on organising small groups.

In other settings it has been more a question of numbers; some churches find they are only in touch with a small number of children, so working with a small group is not an option but a necessity.

These small groups may choose to meet in someone's home rather than in a hall. Here they may function rather like a club – playing games, watching videos, doing crafts, having discussions and so on. Ideally there will be at least two adults involved even in the smallest of groups so that they can share the load and support one another. The group itself should be encouraged to plan its own activities so that it really owns everything that happens rather than being imposed upon by the adults. Again friendships will be the order of the day.

Where these groups are formed not from necessity but by choice then they may function in a wide variety of ways. They may often be peer groups who have a particular interest or simply want to be together. The adults again act primarily as group facilitators and friends. The group itself will plan its own programme, decide when and where it will meet, what it will do and how it will pay for it (a budget may be set by the church). This will help the children to develop their own decision making skills, a sense of responsibility for one another, and even early awareness of budgeting. In the process care must obviously be taken to be aware of the ages and abilities of the group; the older the group the greater the level of responsibility they can be given. Usually such a group need only plan for around six weeks at a time but many function for months, even years. If a church has several such groups then from time to time it may plan larger events like concerts, meals, or fun nights to which several or all small groups are invited. Normally a group will be around five or six in number plus two adults, but it could be slightly smaller or larger.

The philosophy of this style of work and a very full description of its working is given in Mike Breen's excellent book, *Outside In*. It is in a style which is adaptable to all kinds of areas and all sizes of churches, and is capable of continual expansion as more leaders become available. Above all it is entirely relationship-based and has already proved to be effective in terms of seeing children and young people deciding to follow Jesus.

Small groups clearly also have a function when working with children who have particular learning or relationship difficulties. They can work with the mentally handicapped, the deaf, the blind and the emotionally disturbed. Wherever possible a policy of integration of children designated as 'special needs' ought to be adopted, but there are times and situations in which specific groups for them can have a valid place. These are likely to be best run as small groups.

Finally, small groups can provide a context for children who want to explore more carefully the Christian faith, either out of interest or because they have made some kind of commitment and want to take this further. Such small groups for discovery and nurture are often best run in a home, and can use the same principles as other small groups but with a specific agenda. We will examine these more closely in the closing chapter.

CONCLUSIONS

For ongoing work that aims to help children from non believing families hear about and respond to the Good News of Jesus, midweek activities run alongside the essential core of day to day befriending of families and individual children appear to make the most sense. I would certainly not rule out an ongoing role for Sunday groups for children from both believing and non believing families; where they are run well they have a very important function. But for the 85% who are never seen on a Sunday, midweek groups are likely to be of more value. These groups will vary in style enormously, from larger clubs to very small groups. Some will be very general, others very particular, and they will cover a number of age ranges. The common threads will be a genuine love for all the children involved, a commitment to the wider family wherever possible, friendship and a desire to share Jesus by word and deed.

| ACTIVITIES |

1 How aware is your church of its responsibilities for befriending people from household to household, at the school gate, or over the garden fence as the core way of sharing the good news rather than through organised events?

2 Consider what organised activities are already on offer regularly in your church.

Are they reaching 'non-church' children? If not, why not, and what changes might be needed?

3 Do any of the ideas suggested in this chapter appeal to you as possible ways forward? If so think through whether or not this might be a right direction for you to take.

4 Has this chapter inspired you to think of something quite different? Why not share this with someone and see if it makes any sense. You could even help the author in his development!

| **FURTHER READING** |

Help! There's a Child in My Church! Peter Graystone, Scripture Union, 1989

Help! I Want To Tell Kids About Jesus, Steve Hutchinson, Scripture Union Missions Department, 1988

Outside In, Mike Breen, Scripture Union, 1993

Springboard, Sue Clutterham and Denise Trotter, Scripture Union, 1989

That's a Good Idea, NCEC, 1992

Launchpad, Sue Clutterham, Scripture Union, 1992

Leading a Kid's Club in Your Church, Vernon Cracknell, JBCE, 1990

THE SPECIALS

It is the week in, week out work of befriending children which needs to be at the heart of all children's evangelism. However, there can also be great value in holding special events from time to time. Here we are not concerned with mega-sized special events such as 'Rainbow Special' or 'Bubble Trouble' which took place during the Luis Palau Mission to London in 1982 and the Billy Graham Mission '89. These really are different in scale and budget from anything a local church could envisage. (They had around 17,000 and 19,000 children and adults attending and gave a great boost to the ongoing life of these missions.) Our concern rather is with events such as holiday clubs, weekend specials and term time weeks (sometimes referred to as 'missions'). It could also include some of the single events such as 'Family Praise' parties or 'Family Fun Nights' dealt with in the chapter, 'For All the Family'.

Special events like these need to be much prayed for, carefully planned and prepared; they should also fit in with the overall evangelistic strategy of the local church, and be properly budgeted for. They should never be a substitute for regular ongoing work or without care being taken in follow up. Care should always be taken to make these 'family' events and not for children only.

A NOTE ON EVANGELISTIC STRATEGY

Too many churches do not give serious consideration to developing an overall strategy for their outreach work. As well as enabling individuals and households to see how important it is that they make

Jesus known through their daily lives by building friendships in the community, each church needs to look at what particular activities would be appropriate for it to run. When this is done then Playgroups, Parent and Toddler groups, uniformed organisations, midweek clubs, home groups, visiting programmes, social action groups and so on are all placed in the wider context of a church's strategy. Even where churches have undertaken mission audits and produced outreach strategies, often children's work is not included or is not seen as an integral part of the work. This needs to change. Reaching children needs to be part of the overall strategy of a local church. A good way to start would be for the church leadership to read and discuss *All God's Children?* or to use the 'Decade Strategy Pack' produced by Steve Hutchinson. Whichever you choose do, seek to place any special events within the context of a wider strategy.

TERM TIME WEEKS

These generally last for one week though they might only be for three or four days, or for as long as a fortnight. As children are at school the club-style events will be held either soon after the school day finishes or in the early evening. There may be more than one session. For example, if school ends at 3.15 then there might be a session for five to seven year olds from 3.30 – 4.30 followed by a session for eight to eleven year olds from 4.45 – 6.00. On some evenings there may also be events for teenagers and for the whole family. On the other hand there might simply be one session for all ages from 3.30 – 4.30 or 4.45 or 5.00; or the organisers may decide not to organise anything for either the younger or older age bands and concentrate all efforts on one particular grouping. It may also be more appropriate to run early evening sessions (say, 6.00 – 7.00) rather than something immediately after school.

These after-school sessions could have a jazzy name and ought to be fairly fast-paced. Inside an hour there could be singing, small group times, a quiz, a Bible story (told in various ways), drama, video clips, prayer, games and a memory Bible verse. There might be puppets, karaoke, beat the clock games, soapbox opportunities, interviews, aerobics, news items, birthday celebrations, team challenges, simple craft activities, a serial story, jokes, clowns, short visual talks, and even moments of quiet and stillness.

The whole programme should be great fun, yet have a serious message and involve everyone, but force no one to do anything they are unhappy to do. It should relate to the children's own world and encourage children and adults to develop friendships with each other as the week progresses. The whole programme could explore a biblical theme. Only rarely should there be any behaviour or discipline problems because the children have no time to be bored and are never patronised (the two most common causes of disruptive behaviour). Parents should be welcome to stay throughout, or come back early to join in the final minutes, to ask any questions of the leaders that they like and be invited (ideally personally) to the family events which are included in the week.

During the day, work should be undertaken in the local schools if at all possible. This could involve taking assemblies or lessons or both. Any such work must clearly fit in with the law and be with the full agreement of the headteacher (see the chapter on Schools). This has some clear advantages. First, it should enhance links between the local Christians and the school. Second, it means that every child in a district is being met, receiving some positive input about the Christian faith, and being made aware of the special events happening during that week. This often means higher numbers at the after-school events and in particular tends to attract many more non-church children than other events.

Very often this type of special event takes place with a visiting children's evangelist or even a small team. This adds an extra dimension to the specialness of the event and supplies the church with someone to work solely on school visits and so on during that week. A visitor should also bring fresh ideas, impetus and training, but they should always work in very close association with the local church. No itinerant evangelist should simply arrive with a package and dump it on the local church. They need to listen carefully and learn about the local setting and needs. For the period of consideration, preparation, planning, event and follow up the visitor should be a partner with the local church. If they are not they are failing to serve the church and equip the saints for the work of ministry, thus failing to fulfil their God given calling (cf Ephesians 4:11ff).

Even when the main leader or the person upfront is a visiting evangelist, local people should make up the vast bulk of the team. They have been around before and will still be there when the evangelist has gone. It is far more important in the long run that local people develop friendships with the children and their families than that the evangelist does (though they must not stay aloof from this either). Indeed whilst very often weeks such as these only happen with a visiting evangelist from Scripture Union, Church Army, diocesan or denominational staff or any other organisation, there is no reason why they should not be run locally using local gifts and personnel.

Family events in weeks like these might include a 'Family Fun Night' or a 'Family Presentation' evening. It may be better to hold an event on Saturday afternoon rather than an evening. Sometimes a special Family Service will be run on the Sunday. These, to be honest, receive mixed responses. Sometimes they are well attended, especially if it is a special Sunday anyway (eg Mothering Sunday or Harvest), but sometimes churches have expressed their disappointment at the low turn out of non-church families. This is because coming to a church service is simply too big a leap. It really is time that we grasped just how alien going to church has become to the vast bulk of people, in the Western world at least. For me this fact only further highlights the importance of developing friendships out in the community rather than always expecting 'them' to come to 'us'.

During term time weeks other events may be arranged for children's parents – Men's Suppers held in local pubs, coffee mornings, tea time events or special lunches for those not at work, evenings on parenting issues, or a series of 'meals with a meaning' in peoples homes. These are just a handful of events which have been tried and tested as part of such weeks.

More and more churches are experimenting with term time events along these lines. If we are to reach everyone with the Good News of Jesus then it is likely that this is a direction many more should follow over the next few years.

HOLIDAY CLUBS

The name tells it all. These are events arranged during school
holidays. Any school holiday can be appropriate – half terms,
Christmas, summer or Easter. They are certainly most popular in
the summer because the weather is more likely to be kind; the
holiday is longer and often more people are available to help.
However, there are some real plus points about using other times
of the year. Often at half terms there is no local authority provision;
in the summer there are always some people away on holiday whereas
at half terms, especially in February, this is less common. Follow up
is often easier following events in half terms or shorter school holidays
especially as so many churches in the UK close many activities down
in August. If a club is arranged for the end of a holiday period then
advertising is often more difficult as children tend to forget about
events they are told about in mid July which don't actually happen
until the end of August. All such factors need to be weighed up when
considering the timing of special events.

Holiday clubs do have one great bonus over term time events. It
is possible to have much more time with the children. Generally
holiday clubs run for a week though some may choose to operate for
a fortnight or only a few days. They will run for mornings only
(usually 2–2½ hours), afternoons only or all day, either with a lunch
break or children bringing sandwiches with them. Some run evening
events as well, which are often geared towards the 11 plus age groups.
Once again there should be strong family elements in the overall
programme, similar to the term time events.

During a holiday club many elements will be very like those of the
term time club. However, with more time available there is much
greater scope for including a wider range of craft activities which can
be done at a more demanding level. Through the week children
should be able to have a go at a variety of crafts including clay
modelling, painting, drama workshops, mime, music making, scraper
boards, collage, montage, 'junk' modelling, radio making, video
workshops, computer skills, woodwork, ecology workshops, fabric
painting, paper quilling, jewellery making, puppets, papier mache,
plaster casting, cookery, kite making, needlework, pyrography, and
so on. These require a reasonable amount of time in a programme

to be done well. Some are very cheap, others less so, but it is worth having a decent budget so that you can offer a good range and standard. All crafts should be done in small groups so that relationships can be built up. Small group times to chat about a Bible story or do a funsheet together can generally be longer in a holiday club context. It is important, however, not to let the programme drag. Keep the whole event moving.

With more time available, too, a range of special events could be included: outings, visiting performers, meals and so on. Increasingly churches are becoming happy to run holiday clubs on their own. There tends to be more help available in school holidays and there is now a very good range of published programmes for holiday clubs produced by Scripture Union and others (eg *Secret Agents, Scarecrows, J Team, Light Factory*, and *Shipshapes*). But many churches also invite itinerant children's evangelists to help them with holiday clubs, either to get them started or for fresh impetus. It is unhealthy, however, to develop a great dependence on such visitors. After each visit careful thought should be given as to whether or not next time it should be either a different visitor, or better, locally run. One possible pattern for a church beginning to use holiday clubs might be for a visitor to lead it in Year 1; to jointly lead it with locals in Year 2; for locals to lead it in Year 3 with the visitor acting as advisor so that in Year 4 there is no need for the visitor at all. In this way the evangelist is not just 'here today and gone tomorrow', but equips the saints to do the work. Where a local church does use published materials care needs to be taken. However good the materials are they need to be adapted to a local setting. Use them as the heart of the programme by all means but do not feel totally bound to them or by them. Then, after using them for a year or two, why not see if you can produce your own programme. Go on, be creative!

Some churches may opt to run holiday activities in different ways. Some may run a straightforward playscheme which includes craft activities as in a holiday club but without specific Christian teaching. The emphasis is entirely on offering a service to the local community and building relationships with the children and families who come. This is a perfectly valid way of working. Churches operating in this way may want to consider how they are actually telling the Good

News to people, and whether it is happening on the scheme through conversations. But if they are clear that this is the best way to operate in their area then it is surely good.

Others may decide not to run events which bring large numbers of children together, but instead to run a large number of small group activities simliar to those described in the previous chapter. The only difference will be that rather than meeting weekly they will meet daily, or every other day perhaps, for a week, fortnight or even for the whole summer. This avoids the problems associated with large numbers of children gathering together, and again establishes the base for forming relationships to the whole event. It can also be sustained over longer periods of a holiday because it is less energy sapping in terms of preparation and control. On the debit side it could lose out on the fun, excitement and possibilities that operating on a larger scale can bring.

The other holiday option is of course to take the kids away. That has a chapter all to itself.

WEEKEND SPECIALS

Some churches might feel that a whole week, or anything midweek, is simply not viable for them. So why not organise a special weekend? An event on Friday evening and then all day on Saturday can be superb.

One option would be to take some of the published holiday club materials and treat the weekend as a short club using three days of material, or produce your own, of course.

Another option would be to hold a barbecue or meal or a presentation on Friday evening followed by a day of stories, games, and crafts on the Saturday, all based around a Bible theme or story.

Another option would be to make it a genuinely family weekend with people of all ages present throughout doing all sorts of creative things together. The type of events organised can be identical to those already covered under 'term time', 'holiday clubs' and 'For All The Family', but simply put into a weekend period.

MAKING IT KNOWN

Whatever types of event we organise as specials we will want to make them known to the wider community. If their purpose is to share the Good News of Jesus with those outside the church we have to deem them failures if only church folk are there or if the place is packed with non-church people and the church people have opted out entirely (the latter being a less likely scenario). Publicity will be important, and well produced posters and invitations are required. Get these out where people are, on school notice boards, outside the school gate (ask permission first), in local community centres, and from door to door. If visits into the school are possible then ask permission to distribute invites after assembly or lessons.

'Stunt' style publicity like driving around with loudspeakers mounted on a car (like politicians at election time), parachute games in the market place, street theatre and so on could be used as well (make sure you have any necessary permission for these). But the most crucial publicity is by word of mouth as children ask their friends, neighbours invite neighbours, people at work invite their colleagues, and it is made clear that all are welcome. Here often is the real rub. So many Christians do not have real contact with many non Christians. We need to help each other change this situation.

We need to consider too the suitability of venues. Neutral territory, eg local schools, or even regular territory for non Christians will often be better than church buildings. Sometimes a marquee in the local park may be best. Venue may be less of a problem with children than with adults. Church halls are obviously better than church sanctuaries for most events mentioned in this book, especially if the church makes their buildings available as a community resource on a regular basis rather than hog the buildings to itself. Parent and toddler groups, playgroups, nurseries, dancing classes, uniformed organisations like Cubs or Guides, luncheon clubs, drop in centres, sports clubs, keep fit, games and quiz nights, first aid sessions, local councillors surgeries, bazaars, jumble sales and so on are all ways in which such facilities might be used. In this way a wider number of non-church folk know that it is okay to be in these premises and that they are safe places for their children to be in.

Finally, on making it known, it is underhand to advertise events which will include Christian teaching without making that clear in the publicity. Make the publicity bright, attractive and fun, but make sure it is totally clear and honest too.

CONCLUSIONS

Special events are great fun and can be very rewarding. They do tend to attract non-church children and adults if they are organised, publicised and run well. They can do a great deal for the local church's credibility in the local community as well as be vehicles which God can use to bring people of all ages to faith in Christ.

They also take up a lot of time and energy. If careful thought is not given as to how they fit in with the overall outreach strategy and the wider, regular work of reaching children and families then they can become like a firework, suddenly alight and bright while it lasts but over in a flash and lost in the memory. Make your specials really good events that will have a lasting effect on people's lives.

| ACTIVITIES |

1 Does your church have an overall outreach strategy? If YES: How does the work with children and families fit into this?

If NO: To whom do you need to talk to begin to bring a strategy into being?

2 Consider any special activities you have held. Did they fit into an overall strategy? What was really good about them? What lasting effects have they had?

3 Find a nearby church planning a special event and arrange to visit, observe and learn from it.

4 Prayerfully consider organising a special event in six months time. If it seems right to you and the Holy Spirit, go for it!

| FURTHER READING |

Mission: Possible, Malcom Egner, Scripture Union, 1990

The Well-Church Book, John Finney, Scripture Union, 1991

Decade Strategy Pack, Steve Hutchinson, Scripture Union Missions Department, 1991

Know How To Run a Holiday Club, David Savage, Scripture Union Missions Department, 1992

Foward in Faith and *Angels on the Move* (mission audit resources which include children), Southwell Diocese, 1990

INTO SCHOOLS

In the past few years there has been a near explosion in the numbers of Christians involved in schools work. Organisations like Scripture Union, British Youth For Christ, and Schools Outreach have led the way, alongside the longstanding role of diocesan education officers in Church of England schools. But there are many smaller local organisations involved plus numerous ministers, vicars, pastors and local church teams. This work has been in both primary and secondary schools; county (often referred to popularly as state), voluntary controlled and aided (mainly church but also Jewish and Muslim) and independent schools are all covered.

The growth has come about for a number of reasons. First, very many have been concerned at the decline of teaching on Christianity in Religious Education even though the 1988 Education Reform Act requires that RE is taught to all pupils and that it should be 'mainly, broadly Christian'. This concern has not come only from Christian parents, but also from many who do not profess the Christian faith themselves. To help rectify this people have felt that specialist schools workers would be of value. Second, there has been a concern that even where Christianity is taught it is often done so unsympathetically by non believing teachers. Third, it has been recognised that school is the one place where nearly all the 5–16 year olds in this country can be found on a regular basis. If we are to 'go where people are', then to meet children we need to go to the schools.

It is not the place of this book to examine these reasons in any detail; this has been done fully elsewhere. It is important, however, that we do look at the practical ways in which Christians can be involved in local schools of whatever sort they may be. It is also my personal conviction that we should be involved.

PRAYER

Prayer has to undergird any of the work mentioned in this book but in some settings it may be the only thing that can be done for a local school, at least initially. Parents with children at school ought to pray not only for their own children at school but also for the others, their parents, teachers and other staff at the school. Those who have no children can also join in praying for schools. Local schools should be regularly prayed for in church services and prayer meetings. If schools in your area do not have a group praying for them, why not begin one yourself?

HELPING IN SCHOOL

In primary schools especially there are often many ways in which parents can help. (Though you do not have to be a parent to offer to help, it is likely that you will have to go through a vetting procedure before being accepted if you are not.) You can help by going into school for an hour or two each week to listen to children read, or read to them; you can help them with their writing, or with sewing, cutting out, mending text books and a host of other matters. You can also go on trips and assist with escorting and supervising the children. This is all a matter of serving the children and the school. It is about being present as a Christian rather than going in to overtly evangelise. As friendships develop with staff, parents and children you may have the chance to share your faith; if it is a freely asked question, and providing the response is loving and not at all pushy there should be no problems.

Another very specific way that people can become involved in schools is by becoming a school governor. Parents can become parent governors and others might put themselves forward for co-option or, in the case of church schools, be foundation governors. To be a governor is a large scale commitment but means you are involved in helping the school in a very broad way. Christians who take on this role need to make sure that they do so prepared to play their part fully and to seek the best for all involved with the school. They are not there 'to fight the Christian corner', but to seek the welfare of the whole school. When they take on such a role they are being 'salt and light' to this part of the local community. It is a very worthwhile involvement.

ASSEMBLIES AND LESSONS

Whilst helping is an option for just about anyone, taking assemblies and lessons is not. You need to be good at communicating with children to even contemplate doing either of these, and you need to be aware that school is not a place for overt evangelism. You cannot stand in an assembly and call for a response to the gospel; this would be an abuse of privilege and a quick guarantee that you would not be invited back. This does not mean that assemblies and lessons need to be bland or a watered down version of the Christian faith. It is quite legitimate to state plainly what Christians believe, or what you believe personally, so long as it is done in a way which respects the faiths and convictions of others and does not insist on acceptance of these stated Christian beliefs. It is perfectly legitimate to tell a Bible story (as a story, sketch or video etc) but not to say 'and this means you must / need to'. Allow the story to stand on its own. Actually this is regularly what Jesus did anyway. He told a story and left it up to the hearers to decide what it meant or what response they should make. The gospel writers who retell the events regularly allow the reader to apply it to their own situations. Such is the power of good stories (and please remember story does not mean *untrue* fable) that power is removed from them as soon as we start to explain them.

In assemblies we need to be very thoughtful about the words of any songs that we sing. Many popular Christian worship songs may be very lively and enjoyable, but they are often hard for children to understand and may be asking children from other faiths to sing things they do not believe. Just imagine your own child came home singing a worship song from another faith group; how would you feel?

We also need to take care about prayer. To pray 'in Jesus' name' may not be the best use of words in a setting where children do not know what this means and where for them it is to utter a blasphemy. To use quiet prayer or to talk to God simply may be more appropriate. The recitation of the phrase 'in Jesus' name' is not a magic incantation granting a guaranteed answer to our prayers. God knows the heart from which our prayers come; it is in that sense that our prayers need always to be offered in the name of the one Lord, Jesus.

In the setting of a church school some of these precautionary words need not apply, though even here I am convinced that respect and sensitivity should mark all that we do, as many children will come from families where the Christian faith is not owned.

In taking lessons it is important to remember the principles of the way children learn and the normal practice of work in schools. Make sure the children are involved. Respect their comments and views. Answer their questions honestly and carefully. Help them to learn by doing rather than simply stand at the front and talk to them. Lessons may not be about the Bible and Christian faith. It will often be better to be dealing with a moral or social question and to come to that from a Christian viewpoint. However you may just want to help out at a games afternoon for a change.

Schools are rightly concerned not to allow just anyone through their doors to be involved. They have a duty to the children and their parents to offer the best education they can. Any Christians wanting to help with lessons and assemblies must make sure they offer the very best in educational terms. They must also ensure good relations with the headteacher and be willing to listen to any guidelines that the head wishes to lay down, and keep to them. It is, after all, the headteacher's responsibility to ensure that educationally the school is well run.

SCHOOL GROUPS

In many schools there are Christian groups which meet at lunch time or straight after school, with the permission of the headteacher. These can be run by teachers, ancillary staff, parents, local church members and the children themselves. They can be called almost anything; Christian Union, Scripture Union, Bible Club, Quest Club, God Squad, and The Crew are amongst the names I have come across. These groups function in a variety of ways, including singing, prayers, Bible reading, Bible study, speakers, quizzes, videos, games, expert panels, funsheets or drama, though never all these in one session. These groups help Christian students by offering them support and teaching in the school setting. They also function evangelistically for other children as it is somewhere they can go to learn about the Christian faith with their peers. It is on their territory and not the church's. Churches would do well to pray for more of these groups to be established and to support them wherever they exist. Allow the children to do as much of the organising and leading as possible. This experience will help them to develop their own gifts for the present and the future. These groups can gain a great deal of support, too, by being linked up with Scripture Union in Schools.

GETTING STARTED

From time to time training events are held for people wanting to start work in schools, or to develop their skills further. If you come across such an opportunity, grab it. People can get started in a variety of ways. In all these situations it is well worth contacting someone like Scripture Union in Schools to ask for advice and help.

1   Start praying for a school yourself, and perhaps start a prayer group.
2   Parents may be asked to help out in the school, so accept the invitation. But if no request is made it will do no harm to offer to help.
3   When elections for parent governors come around, or if the school or local authority advertises for people interested in being co-opted governors, then look into this possibility seriously.
4   Encourage any Christian children in a school to think about starting a Christian group, and offer to help them.
5   If you think you have the skills needed for assemblies and lessons it is probably wise to check it out with someone else first (unless you are a trained teacher already). Ministers in particular should not

assume that because they are 'ordained' they can take assemblies; many of the worst assemblies have been conducted by the local vicar or minister. If you are still sure, then it does no harm to politely and gently approach the headteacher, or sometimes the head of a particular section. They may well respond warmly to your offer. If they do, make sure your first visit goes well. If you step out of line you will not only mess up the future for yourself but you may well do so for others too.

6   Seriously consider using school premises for your regular midweek club, term time special, or holiday club. They will almost certainly be better equipped than your church hall. They are neutral territory and should have safe play areas to use. The one drawback may be the cost.

Christians were largely responsible for the establishment of schools in many countries of the world. They remain places where Christians should be present acting as 'salt and light' to the community. We should certainly be 'in the schools'.

| ACTIVITIES |

Take the six points under 'Getting Started' and consider any appropriate action you could, or even should, take.

| FURTHER READING |

Leading Worship in Schools, Janet King, Monarch Publications, 1990

On Track, Termly magazine for primary school groups produced by Scripture Union in Schools.

For material published in Australia contact Scripture Union National Office, 241 Flinders Lane, Melbourne 3000

| CHAPTER |
| TWELVE |

TAKING THE KIDS AWAY

We opened this book with the true story of a letter from someone, now in their late teens, making a clear commitment to Christ. If you remember, she traced the roots of her learning of Christ to the camps she attended when she was aged nine to eleven. Time and again I meet people, now in early adulthood, who vividly recall their times away on Christian holidays. Their experience had been terrific and had a long lasting impact on their lives.

In the summer of 1991 at a camp for eight to eleven year olds I was talking to a girl who had already been on a skiing holiday in the winter and had just returned from Disneyworld before coming on the camp at Longbarn. The camp is in many senses rudimentary; chemical loos, sleeping on the ground in tents, no electricity and no fancy equipment. But there is a lot of open space; there are trees to climb, streams to jump in, tyres to swing on, a camp fire, sleeping out under the stars, forty-nine other children and around twenty adult leaders. I asked her which holiday had been best. 'This one,' she said very definitely. 'Why?' I asked. 'Is it because it is the one you are on now?' 'Oh no,' she responded. 'This is the best one because it's the most exciting!'

Later that same summer a leader from a camp for eleven to thirteen year olds was talking with me about how they had seen God at work in the lives of many of these young people during the camp. 'Do you know,' she said, 'several of those children told me that they had come to know Jesus at Longbarn in the previous two years. They came from both church and non-church families and here they all were, going on with God.'

Both incidents warmed my heart enormously. They reaffirmed the value of 'taking the kids away'.

THE VALUE OF RESIDENTIAL EVENTS

Going away for a weekend, a few days, or a week has a number of clear values. But first a word of caution. Just as special events need to be part of an ongoing regular programme of work to be of real lasting value, so do residential events. This is true whether it be a child or group of children going off on a holiday organised by Pathfinders, Falcon Camps, Crusaders, Scripture Union or any other organisation, or if it is a locally arranged event. There needs to be continuity in the work with every child.

This continuity will differ in form quite markedly from child to child and event to event, but it needs to happen. If it is a locally arranged weekend away, say, then it will be part of the overall programme for that group of children. If it is a group of children going to an organised camp then either they will be going because of a connection somewhere to a local group or a caring Christian family, or the leaders of the activity will stay in touch through the year via letter, Christmas and birthday cards, phone and reunion events.

The most obvious value of residentials is time. Instead of having the children for a couple of hours once or twice a week, as in a regular club setting, they are with you twenty-four hours a day for as long as you are away. This is wonderful for building up good relationships because relationships take time. It means you have to work harder at those relationships because inevitably it is not always plain sailing. Children will push you to see what you are really like; they will tease you, try your patience, step out of line, argue, sometimes fight and generally make life hard for you! They are also great fun to be with, highly cooperative, interesting people and caring; they will teach you things, they will be appreciative. However, unless you are ready for the negatives do not get stuck into residentials. You have to take the rough as well as the smooth. You have to make the effort for the awkward child, the one you find you don't like, the one you are tempted to thump, otherwise you are not doing your job.

The flip side to getting to know children better because you are with them for twenty-four hours a day (and sometimes it really does feel like you haven't had any sleep!), is that they can get to know you better too. Any veneer you manage to keep up for two hours at club will be stripped away on a camp. The reality of what you speak about Jesus will be tested by the way you live. In other words, being away for a few days creates an opportunity for children to experience the reality of our faith as well as be taught about it.

It is likely that on any time away more time than is possible in other contexts is given to direct Christian teaching. It can be as varied and lively as at other times in its presentation but may offer the chance to look at issues in more depth. Beware of making any residential a highly spiritual hothouse, however. It may well seem wonderful at the time but in the cold light of life back at home it may prove to be very ephemeral. What seemed like a mighty anointing of God on a meeting at camp might be looked back on as emotional fervour leading to nothing. Rather there should be a balance of activities and a naturalness about the way Jesus is shared.

I recall two houseparties, both for ten to thirteen year olds, both mixed, both with myself as the speaker. After the final evening of the first a very gentle appeal was made for people interested in becoming Christians to stay behind at the end of the session whilst everyone else left to get their evening drink. Around twenty-five stayed out of fifty. We talked a little more, individual leaders chatted to the young people and it was later reported that all twenty-five had become Christians. On the second occasion no appeal was made. Instead an invitation was given to meet at eight o'clock the next morning before breakfast if anyone was seriously interested in following Christ. Fifteen were there next morning. A similar procedure was followed, but the report this time was of seven or eight becoming Christians, three making a fresh commitment and the others going away feeling they needed to think about it all a bit more before deciding.

In a newsletter or press release to the Christian world I know, sadly, which one would have gained the bigger billing and which would have brought more invitations for work. Thankfully God does not operate in the same way. Of the twenty-five very few are now serious about God. Of the fifteen nearly all remain so, perhaps most strongly those who went away to think further.

Sometimes, when preparing leaders for camp, a colleague and I say to the team, 'If you want them all converted, we'll do it tonight. If you want real followers of Jesus, then let's be gentle, thoughtful and allow the children and, above all, the Holy Spirit the time they need.' If you recall the children mentioned earlier who said they had become Christians at Longbarn camp then you may not now be surprised to hear that this was real news to the leaders of Longbarn. No big appeals had been made. The gospel had been gently explained and the children encouraged to think for themselves about Jesus. Their 'decisions', which they told a year or two later, had been made quietly on their own without any reference to an adult or any serious counselling session. But the Holy Spirit had been at work.

Residentials can be camps in tents, or purpose built cabins; they might be at residential centres, in schools, hotels, conference centres, even private homes. They may have very specific programmes such as horse riding, go karting and sailing holidays, or they may be more general in their activities. For all there are some very important practical guidelines.

PRACTICAL GUIDELINES

1 Leadership
It is vital that any residential activities are well led. There will need to be an overall leader or leadership team, and a good team. The ratio of leaders to children will differ a little depending on the nature of the holiday. All the holidays I am involved in seek to have a ratio of one adult to three children as a minimum. If we can be one to two I am happier.

All leaders need to be suitable people (as with all activities) and undergo appropriate training.

2 Tasks
On the team you need a qualified First Aid person. If you are ever going swimming you ought to have at least one qualified life saver. Your cook and caterer (this may be more than one person) need to be good, and ensure that they operate within the Food Safety Act

1990. You need to be clear who will act as overall pastoral leaders to the team.

3 Insurance
Make sure you are properly insured for every aspect of the holiday.

4 Procedures
Have clear emergency procedures in the event of fire, flood, storm etc. Also have clear procedures if a child either discloses abuse or is suspected of abuse. Never try to be the social worker!

5 Budget
Make sure you budget properly so that you cover all your costs.

6 Health
Children going on a residential need parental permission to go in the first place. You should also require every parent to submit a full health certificate for their child.

7 Parents
Make sure parents know where you are, how to contact you in emergencies, know when and where their children will be returned, are aware of the nature of the holiday, have given permission for their child to be with you and take part in all activities, have completed a health form for their child. You, naturally, should be happy to tell the parents anything they would like to know about the holiday and the content of the Christian teaching.

8 Age
As a guide I have never taken children under 8 away on a separate children's holiday. Under the Children Act 1989 any holidays which include children under 8 apart from their parents will have to be properly registered. On family holidays any ages should be welcome.

Family residentials
Children's camps and holidays are run all over the world. Many will testify to the role these have played in their spiritual development. Many non-church children love being on them, find they learn much

about God through being on them, and some actually come into Christian faith through them.

There really ought to be rather more family camps run around the world. The whole family (whatever its make up) can come, and there are lots of activities, some for all ages to do together, others for children or adults on their own. So there is a good mixture of all-age leisure and learning, and peer group leisure and learning. Together, whole families can discover Christ and develop deeper relationships with each other.

These events may offer a break for families who cannot afford a holiday in a hotel or guest house. They may help families spend time together in a way in which during the normal pressures of life they find impossible to do. Parents and children will learn much about each other. If such events are also open to the childless, the single person, and the elderly then a wonderful experience in community parenting can occur. More churches need to experiment with these events. Many people in local communities may be open to taking part, especially if they are given the freedom to join in only what they want to join in. It will offer them an experience of the Good News rather than lots of words, and the experience will often break through in a way the words never would do.

Local churches probably need to rethink their existing church weekends and holidays to bring such family events about. So often the children are sidelined at church weekends by having their 'own programme' which has no connection to everyone else's programme. Church weekends ought to be truly all-age activities.

FOLLOWING UP ON RESIDENTIALS

Mention was made earlier of the need for residentials to be part of an ongoing programme. If they are run by the local church then this ought to be a straightforward matter – follow up locally. If the event draws from a wider area, however, then as well as putting people in touch with a local church fellowship near them, team members should try and keep in touch with people. Letters, cards and organised reunions are the tried and tested methods. You can also encourage the children to read the Bible regularly and give them suitable notes to help them with this. Encourage children to pray too.

When writing to a child make sure that there is nothing in the letter which you would be uneasy about parents reading. It is important, too, to write to the parents explaining that you would like to keep in touch and what the purpose would be. If the parents refuse permission to do so then do not go against their wishes. No one can stop you continuing to pray for the child. If the child has no contact with Christians back at home, then every effort should be made to change this. It will, however, not always be possible. Here again, ongoing contact through letter, and encouragement to attend reunions and return the following year are very important, alongside prayer. Regular prayer is the best form of follow up.

CONCLUSIONS

Taking the kids away is brilliant. If you have never done it then give it a go. Going away with whole families in both small and larger numbers is also brilliant. Why not plan to do it in the next year?

| ACTIVITIES |

1 Look again at the account of the two houseparties. Why do you think the response happened in each case? What lessons might you learn for your own work?

2 Reconsider the section on family residentials. What do you consider to be the advantages and disadvantages of such events?

| FURTHER READING |

The Temporary Community, Tom Slater, Albatross, 1984

The New Camping Book, Tom Slater, Scripture Union Australia, 1990

COUNSELLING CHILDREN

'Ruth.'

'Yes, Sarah.'

'Ruth. I want to be a friend of Jesus too.'

'That's terrific, Sarah. Sit down and tell me why.'

Ruth's heart had leapt with excitement at Sarah's words. But what did Sarah really mean by them? Ruth knew Sarah too well to assume that they should be taken simply at face value. There could well be more to them than their first hearing suggested. Sarah had been coming along to the club that Ruth ran during the week for several months. Now they were away together at camp with around forty other eight to eleven year olds. Sarah had not always seemed to be enjoying the week; she was very quiet and often appeared to withdraw into herself. As the week had gone on she had begun to tell Ruth some of the things that had happened to her; they were far from pleasant. Life at home for Sarah was not always happy. Arguments, fights, physical abuse and possibly sexual abuse appeared to be a regular part of life, not only for Sarah but also for other members of her family.

So how should Ruth handle this counselling situation now? It had been a long tiring day for both Sarah and Ruth. It was late in the evening and the camp was busy preparing for bed after camp prayers and a roaring camp fire. Ruth acted very wisely. You will notice that her immediate response was very positive. But she did not start by saying much to Sarah, rather she encouraged Sarah to tell her more fully what she meant. As it happened, because it was late, after Ruth had listened for a couple of minutes she said something like this;

'Sarah, I am really glad to hear what you have to say about being Jesus' friend. I think we should talk about it some more, don't you? But it is very late now, so I suggest that you go off to bed and then come and find me in the morning after breakfast so that we can have more time to talk about it properly.'

Sarah readily agreed and went off to bed quite happy. The next morning Sarah did find Ruth; they chatted and Sarah, in her own words, asked Jesus to be her friend forever. In the process Sarah also said more about her difficult life at home. Ruth shared this with the camp leader and the leader of the club to which Sarah went. The three agreed not to tell anyone else and reported it to the NSPCC on their return from camp. Several years later Ruth has moved on, but the club leader and social services are still in regular touch with Sarah and her whole family. It takes years to really see such situations resolved fully, and it requires the expert help of professionals.

BASIC GUIDELINES

This story is true. On a camp or houseparty a child may come to a point in their life where they need to make a clear commitment to Jesus. But this is not the only setting where it may occur; it could happen at an evangelistic event, during a holiday or term time club, after a regular Sunday club, or at home just thinking about Jesus. On the other hand, for some children, perhaps especially for those from Christian homes, there may never be such a clear cut point of commitment; as one good friend says of herself, 'Jesus has always been real to me from as far back as I can remember; there have been real points where I have committed my life to him afresh, but I cannot think of a time when I did not know him as my friend.'

However, when a child does need to express their desire to follow Jesus and approaches an adult to talk about it, what guidelines should the 'counsellor' use?

1 Be positive
Take the child and his or her words seriously. Give the approach a warm response not simply by what you say but preferably with a smile as well. If you are in a setting like a large evangelistic event

where you do not know the child, find out his name and a little about where he comes from; and tell the child a little about yourself, too, before you launch into any specific 'counselling'.

2 Be yourself

When you are in a counselling situation it is important to be natural. God does not expect you to be anyone other than yourself in this or any other situation. God himself has equipped you to serve him. Yes, all of us will say the wrong thing sometimes and feel afterwards that we could have done it better, but always remember that it is the Holy Spirit's work to bring people to faith. We simply have the privilege of being his chosen messengers (John 16:8ff and 2 Corinthians 5:20–6:1).

3 Be discerning

Behind a few words there may lie a more complex situation. The child may be talking to you because he wants attention, or to please you, or because all his friends have done so, or because she wants the free booklet she has been told she will be given (so I never tell them there is a booklet available)! The only way to really discern what is happening in the child is to listen carefully to the child and to the Holy Spirit at the same time.

4 Listen, don't talk

Probably the most common mistake made in any counselling situation is that the counsellor talks too much. We are so keen to share our own story or tell the person being counselled what we think they need to know that we fail to stop and listen to what they really want to talk about. We should simply ask questions which help the child tell us his own needs, such as 'Why do you want to become part of God's family?' or 'What do you know about Jesus?' Normally we need to avoid questions to which the answer is simply 'Yes' or 'No'. We certainly want to avoid putting words into the child's mouth; always let him tell you in their own words. If you are not clear what he is saying, or simply want to make sure you have understood properly, then you can 'replay' the words saying something like, 'I think you are saying that . . . is that right?' But always make sure you are replaying his own words and not introducing new ones. As you are listening to the child's words be aware also of body language. Sometimes the child clearly conveys by her actions that she is not being really serious, whatever her words may be saying. Equally, she may have difficulty finding any words to use at all, but something about her actions can convey real seriousness. Then we must always be listening to the inner voice of God's Spirit; he alone truly knows what is going on in the child's mind and will. After all, giving and growing faith is his work not ours.

5 Mind your language

Children's language is generally more limited than that of adults. This is true in terms of both vocabulary and ideas. As we have seen earlier children tend to think in very 'concrete' terms; 'abstract' ideas are largely foreign to them, and even when they do begin to grasp 'abstract' ideas they tend to do so in short bursts and revert to 'concrete' terms most of the time. So most children will not understand religious terminology like 'salvation', 'judgment' or 'atonement'. Indeed many will not understand 'sin', 'crucifixion' or 'resurrection'. We must use words they will understand; so, for example, rather than salvation we might talk about God rescuing us; rather than crucifixion we will talk about being put to death on a cross.

When it comes to ideas we need to use word pictures which connect with the world of the child. 'Sin' is a concept many adults have not grasped. The heart of 'sin' is turning away from God; because we have turned away or rebelled we commit sins. Somehow we need to communicate this to children. Rather than 'committing sins' we can talk about 'doing wrong things like being unkind or lying'; this should help a child understand the idea of 'committing sins' pretty quickly. But to communicate the heart of sin as turning away will need the use of 'concrete' images like that of turning around from following God's way to go on our own way, or breaking the friendship by saying, 'I don't want to be your friend anymore.'

Likewise when it comes to talking about 'becoming a Christian' we should take great care with our language. If a highly intelligent Jewish teacher and leader had difficulty grasping what 'being born again' meant we should not be surprised if a child finds it beyond their scope as well. (I would add here that although this has become a very common picture used by evangelicals it is not a very common one in the New Testament; apart from the story of Nicodemus in John 3, it only occurs in Titus 3:5 and 1 Peter 1:3, 23. There are also a handful of references to being born of God without the 'again', but these are only found in John's writings apart from James 1:18.) However, children already have clear ideas about 'friends' and 'families' and 'following'. All three of these ideas are pictures that the Bible uses for becoming Christian. We are made 'God's friends' (Romans 5:10); we become 'God's children' (Romans 8:14) and therefore part of his family; Jesus called his first disciples with the words, 'Follow me.' Here then are three biblical images accessible to the world of the child. They are picture images we can and should use with children when counselling them about becoming Christians. Indeed they are images that are of value not simply for the initial step of faith but for the whole of our Christian pilgrimage. Further, they are images which avoid an over emphasis on conversion as a crisis rather than a process. At some point life begins for a foetus, a friendship begins, or following a leader or team commences, but it is not always possible to pinpoint that beginning in one's own mind. So too with faith. Many people can say clearly, 'I am in God's family,' but cannot pin down a time or place of birth. This surely does not matter; it is the fact that they know they belong and are continuing to live that out which is crucial, not recalling the moment of birth. This is true of people of all ages, but I believe it is even more important to keep in mind when working with children.

6 Be above reproach

I remember clearly my own first experience of counselling at a large crusade. I was a teenager and had only been a Christian for a year or two. I attended all the preparation classes, learnt the verses, underlined them in my Bible and made sure I had practised filling out the referral cards several times; they seemed so complicated. Then came the crusade, and when the call was given I began walking forward during the second verse of the hymn as I had been instructed to do. There already at the front was a boy of, I guessed, twelve. After the evangelist had spoken to those who had come forward for a few minutes we all left the large hall and went through to a room behind the stage to begin counselling. It was packed solid. I began talking to the boy and asked him to explain why he had come forward. I made plenty of mistakes: I forgot his name, talked too much and did not listen carefully enough. Yet it seemed that God had spoken to him and he prayed the prayer on the counselling card. It never crossed my mind that he had probably come with an adult who might be waiting for him and wondering what on earth was going on in this room that he could not see or get near as no one was allowed through to it without a counsellors badge.

Twenty years on I have to say that times have changed quite markedly. Looking back I am not at all sure that this arrangement was particularly wise then; today I believe it would be disastrous. Our world has become much more alert to the reality of abuse of children. Taking them off into a separate room out of view of both adults and other children, even in a group, to me no longer seems right. To do so with an individual child would be even worse. Why do I say this? As followers of Jesus surely we should seek always to be above reproach. If we act openly for all to see then we reduce the dangers of appearing to favour children who 'respond' over against those who do not. We reduce the dangers, too, of being accused of pressurising or even physically mishandling the children we counsel. I say only 'reduce' the dangers because I have both seen and been told of too many incidents in which, even in open counselling, adults have pressurised children into 'making decisions'. I have stood on the edge of a large tarpaulin on which scores of children were being counselled by adults and seen a male counsellor put his arms around a young girl; he meant it to be a sign simply of friendship and assurance as she prayed. From where I stood it looked like nothing of the sort. A person standing nearby also noticed and gently approached the man suggesting he remove his arm. He did and all was well, but it need not have been. Men who counsel any girls or women need to be aware of their own vulnerability, and everyone is vulnerable. Likewise when they counsel boys. In case you think I am being over cautious because we are dealing with Christians, please think again. Sadly the statistics show that abuse is just as common amongst Christians as non Christians, and the abuse of emotional pressure is a great temptation for Christian counsellors in their desire to see others join God's family.

So I suggest the following.

1   Whenever possible do all counselling in full view of other people. If the child's parents' are present, personally I would prefer them to be sitting with me throughout any counselling, whether or not they are Christians. However, I always want the child to talk for themselves. Do not allow parents to put words into their child's mouth. Others prefer to counsel the child alone but parents should certainly be close enough to see what is going on. Older children may opt to ask their parents to move away a little; for them it is part of their growing up that they are doing this on their own (anytime from five years old onwards, depending on the maturity of the particular child, but especially likely from eight years old onwards). If parents are not around, then encourage the child to tell them what they have decided to do. Often I suggest they do this not necessarily by rushing home and shouting all about it but rather that they tell their parents by the way they will live as Jesus' friend or follower.

2   Sit close enough to hear and be heard but normally avoid physical contact.

3   Never push a child into making a commitment there and then; if they want to then do not stop them, but always give them the option of thinking further. (So I would say at the end of a conversation where it is clear the child is seriously considering asking Jesus to be their friend, something like, 'Would you like to ask Jesus to be your friend now, or would you rather go home or wait until morning and make up your mind then?')

4   In any follow up, ensure that the child's parents or guardians are aware of why you are in contact with their child and of what you are saying or doing.

5   When you are in a position of being alone with a child for counselling (eg after a Sunday group) try to ensure another adult knows. If this is unavoidable then take even more care to avoid physical contact or any emotional pressure than in an open setting.

I find it deeply saddening that I have to write in such a cautionary way. A child finding faith for the first time, or taking a new step forward in their journey of faith is one of the most exciting things we can ever have the privilege of being involved in. But given the reality of our world today we need to take all the care we can. The evil one would love any excuse to try and get in to mar the whole thing.

FOLLOW UP

Some piece of literature (eg leaflet, booklet or Bible reading notes) may be given as part of the counselling process. Choose this very carefully. It should be something that will help the child on their own at home.

Make contact with the child and their family after the event. If you live close by then visit the home to talk with the parents and give them help about how they could help their child grow in their friendship with God. If you live further away then write to the parents openly and ask their permission to continue contact with the child. Encourage parents to talk with their children, to pray with them, to read the Bible together, to worship together, to be in touch with other Christians together. If they feel unable to do this, or even express opposition then graciously accept it. Do not try and undermine the parent and keep praying regularly for the child. Let me share some stories to show that God can and does keep such children.

I met a man who is now a Christian evangelist but whose background was Hinduism. He heard the stories of Jesus as a child at a Catholic school in India. In time he came to worship Jesus as a god. In adult life when a real personal crisis came to him he found himself crying out to Jesus to help him because he remembered the stories he had been told as a child of Jesus helping people in need. Jesus heard that cry and the man came to see Jesus not simply as a god amongst many but as the one true Lord of all. He wants to spend the rest of his life serving him.

A lady from a similar background has shared, 'I always knew that Jesus was true but until I was old enough to cope with the difficulties that becoming a Christian would create in my family I kept quiet about my beliefs and continued to go to the Temple.' She has now had a very painful break with her family because they disowned her when she was baptised. A Muslim boy once confided in a colleague, 'I still go to the Mosque and say all the prayers. But when I am praying I am thinking of Jesus.' 'That's okay,' responded the colleague, 'I'm sure Jesus understands.'

A girl, who had been trained to steal by her parents, attended a holiday club and really wanted to become a friend of Jesus. She shared this with the leader but added, 'If I become a friend of Jesus then I should stop stealing, shouldn't I?' 'Yes,' said the leader, imagining that the child was thinking only of the occasional bar of chocolate from the sweet shop. 'But then my parents wouldn't love me any more.' 'What do you mean?' Then the whole story came out. The shocked leader tried to assure the girl that she was being over dramatic, but the child never shifted her ground. The leader said, 'Well you go away and think about it.'

The next day the girl returned and with a big smile told the leader, 'I asked Jesus to be my friend at home last night and, you know, I know he is. And I've promised him I will stop stealing.' Sadly the parents did disown their own eight year old daughter when she refused to carry on stealing. They treated her very badly but she would not change her mind. Eventually she was taken into care and then fostered by a Christian family who had been part of the holiday club team and knew the whole story. This true story is particularly tragic as clearly she had never really been loved anyway. Follow up for her meant total commitment by those who had shared Jesus with her in the first place.

For most of us the parent wanting the best for their child will accept that, if their child has decided something about Jesus and it is important to them, then they will help them with it. This is even if the parent(s) themselves do not understand or think, even hope, their child will grow out of it. Most parents will be cooperative if we make it clear that we have no desire to drive a wedge between the child and the family, and really want the very best for the child and the parent.

HANDLING DISCLOSURE OF ABUSE

This is a book in itself. All that is intended here is to paint a big red warning sign. If a child discloses abuse then you must take it seriously. You must listen very carefully and never put words into the child's mouth. Then you must explain to the child that you cannot promise not to tell anyone else; you *can* promise that you will only tell it to the leader of the activity. You must do this because you have a responsibility to report any such disclosures and to keep it as confidential as possible. The overall leader of the activity should then report it carefully to the local social services or the NSPCC.

Under no circumstances should you examine a child to look for signs of abuse, any such examination may actually constitute an abuse in itself. And under no circumstances should you try and play the role of social worker.

Hearing a child tell of abuse is heart rending. You may want to go and confront someone, rip the doors off, all kinds of strong emotional reactions. Your duty is always to the child – remember that and act in their best interests. That means report it. And if you have reason to suspect abuse but the child has not disclosed anything, do not pry. However, if you are really concerned, report it.

CONCLUSIONS

Counselling, understood as a specific skill in helping people understand themselves and their situations, is a very specific role. It is not one that many regular children's workers actually have. It requires proper training and expertise. It covers areas not only of abuse but of bereavement caused through death or divorce, the traumas of family break up, deep rooted fears and so on. The average children's worker needs to know their own limits and where expert help is available if the situation demands it. The thoughts throughout this chapter have been about the normal situations which any children's worker needs to be ready to handle. Please never try and operate out of your own depth.

Counselling, understood as offering the advice and help of a friend, is a skill that all people working with children need to work at and develop. The person who has spent their whole life working with children still has much to learn. The specific situations in which a child wants to take a step forward with Jesus are very exciting for the counsellor. Never let the excitement take over or else there will be a tendency to push, even manipulate the child. Allow the child to speak and decide for themselves. At the end of the day God knows the heart and will of every child. He respects them as people in their own right, so must we.

| ACTIVITIES |

1 In pairs spend a few minutes listening to each other carefully. First 'A' speaks and 'B' listens. 'B' only asks for clarification, and never offers comment. Then 'B' tells 'A' what has been heard. Now reverse roles. It is harder than you think!
2 Take one of the counselling settings given in this chapter and discuss it.

3 What do you make of the basic guidelines? Are there any you would add?
4 Find out about your local, diocesan or denominational counselling services so that you are prepared for when you need them.

| FURTHER READING |

Listen To The Children, A Campbell, Grosvenor, 1979
Helping Children Cope With Grief, R Wells, Sheldon, 1988
Taking Care, Helen Armstrong, National Children's Bureau, 1991
The Wisdom to Listen, Michael Mitton, Grove Books, 1981

Counselling materials

Jesus Loves Me, Scripture Union, 1984

Would You Like to Know Jesus? Scripture Union, 1988
Being God's Friend, Scripture Union Missions Department, 1992
Come and Follow, Cecily Cupit, Scripture Union Australia, 1992
Starting Out, Scripture Union Australia, 1990

LEADERSHIP

All activities with children need good leadership. This means both
good quality leaders and a good ratio of leaders to children. In the
United Kingdom the Children Act 1989 lays down a whole series of
regulations for work involving children under eight years old (see
Appendix for fuller details). These regulations apply to activities that
last for two hours or more. Hence many church activities in the
form of clubs, groups and so on do not fall strictly speaking within
the Act either because they are open only to those eight years old
or over, or because they last for less than two hours. However, many
of the regulations can act as very good guidelines for all our work
with children whether or not they fall within the remit of the Act.

ADULT / CHILD RATIO

A ratio of one adult (ie, eighteen years old, or over) to eight children
is required by the Children Act for some registered activities for
under eights; for others an even smaller ratio may be required by a
local authority. I would personally recommend that the one to eight
ratio is taken as a basic guideline; if at all possible then an even
better ratio than this should be worked, but as a guide for work with
all ages of children it is a good one. In residential events the ratio
should be one adult to two or three children.

QUALITY LEADERS

Having offered such a guideline it is crucial to go on to say that you cannot have just anybody being involved in working with children. It is vitally important that everyone who offers to help is carefully assessed for their suitability. Sadly we have to acknowledge that children's activities in churches are likely to be targets for paedophiles as they will see them as possible places for easy access to children. Unfortunately, voluntary organisations in the UK cannot run formal checks on volunteers through the police checking system. Where an activity for under eights has to be registered then formal vetting will be undertaken by the local authority. But, as already noted, most midweek clubs last for less than two hours and often are for children over eight years old and are therefore excluded from these legal provisions. So churches will need to decide for themselves on the suitability of volunteers. It makes sense to use the criteria used by local authorities under the Children Act. They are as follows.

1 No criminal convictions for offences against children.
2 Previous experience of looking after or working with children is desirable (but, I would add, everyone has to start sometime).
3 Ability to provide warm and consistent care.
4 Knowledge of and attitude to multi-cultural issues.
5 Commitment to treat all children as individuals and with equal concern.
6 Physical health, mental stability, integrity and flexibility.
7 Qualification or training in a relevant field.

The final criteria is perhaps only relevant to the overall leaders of a group; one can hardly expect everyone working with children to have a relevant training qualification. However, all the other criteria could be applied to any leader. Leadership in any Christian sense will involve care for everyone, a desire to treat all equally and fairly, and an overall attitude of service towards others (1 Peter 5:1–4). In working with children this will mean care for all the children with whom we work and for our fellow leaders, along with a commitment to do the best for God and for everyone in the group at every level of their being. Leaders need to listen carefully to God and to those whom they are called to lead. They should seek to see others develop to their full potential, and must be willing not only to lead but also be led when this is appropriate. Good leaders are always learners.

In every situation there is a variety of levels of leadership. There will usually be an overall leader and some assistant leaders, but at different times everyone may find themselves with the responsibility for leading a particular activity or group. If someone is not ready for such a role then care must be taken not to place them in it. However, we should be seeking to help all leaders develop appropriate leadership skills for their own varying roles, and to learn their own limits without ceasing to look for further growth and development in everybody. This will obviously include helping children to develop as leaders themselves.

Working this out practically in each local situation will vary but certain common themes should emerge.

1 Personal profiles
Have a profile on each leader. This should include their personal details, a photo, and a record of both their experience and formal training. Such profiles should be kept up to date and safe so that if any problems arise it is available for any to see.

2 Working agreements
Ideally each leader would have a working agreement with the church. This would cover their commitment to the specific work they are involved in, their responsibilities, an agreement about training, and a commitment to periodic review. Each leader should also be asked to sign a formal declaration that they have had no convictions for offences against children.

3 Training
Training should be a regular part of every leader's life. This could involve attending training run by the local authority, Scripture Union, CPAS or other organisations, or having 'in-house' training, using distance learning materials, or the skills of individual team members. Much training could profitably be done by several churches combining together for training events.

Some areas of training should be mandatory, eg basic child development and care, multi-cultural issues, equal opportunities for children, being part of a team or a basic grasp of biblical principles for working with children. Others may be geared to more individual needs, eg specific craft skills.

At least one person should have some First Aid training, preferably to a St John's or Red Cross level, though it would do no harm for a whole team to undertake a 'Save a Life' course.

Different people in leadership will obviously need different levels of working agreement and training. The overall leader will inevitably have greater responsibilities and wider training needs, but no one should be exempt from the process (least of all the minister)!

This commitment to good leadership and good practice in our work with children will make demands on our time, energies and budgets. Many churches would do well to seriously consider doing less but doing it better. They should ask serious questions about how much money they allocate to children's work so that clubs and the like are adequately resourced and leaders are properly trained. Good children's work does not have to be horrifyingly expensive but neither should it be done on the cheap. This may be something of a revolution in many churches but it must happen. If the overall leadership of the church is not regularly praying for and considering its work with children then there is something deeply wrong. It should be a regular item on all PCC, eldership, and diaconate meetings and a major component in every church's annual budget. The leaders of any children's activities should also take responsibility for ensuring that a number of further very practical provisions are made.

PREMISES AND EQUIPMENT

The property being used for any event needs to be suitable and safe. Again, in the UK the Children Act makes many provisions for the suitability of the property for children's activities. These include provision of adequate toilet facilities, adequate lighting and heating, and the overall safety of equipment being used. These should be natural considerations for any children's activities. Rickety stairs, insanitary toilets, peeling paintwork, low level unguarded heaters, rough wooden floors and the like, are all a danger to the safety of children and should either be dealt with or the property not used. Care needs to be taken that children cannot rush in and out of the premises onto the road. It is best if every property is voluntarily submitted to the Fire Officer for a fire certificate. This will give a maximum number of people for each property, state what fire extinguishers and fire exits should be provided and where they should be placed, and it will require emergency lighting. Once obtained these fire safety standards need to be carefully observed. Every precaution that can be taken should be.

When considering equipment for games, activities and craft, thought should be given to children's safety. Play equipment should be properly assembled, and paints, glue, felt tips, scissors and so on should be child-safe. When involved in something like woodwork, where potentially dangerous tools are in use, every care must be taken to ensure children know how to use the tools properly and that they are supervised to ensure that they do.

FOOD AND DRINK

If food and drink are being provided at any event always avoid additives in the ingredients, even if it means that it costs more. All food should be prepared properly and presented well. Consider the dietary requirements of all who might come. Are there any on special diets, eg vegetarians, kosher or halal meat, no pork? Leaders need to be aware of the beliefs and practices regarding food of all those present and take these into their consideration, eg Jews, Muslims, Sikhs, Hindus, Rastafarians. For the sake of children's teeth avoid sweets as much as possible. If you want to give prizes find better alternatives like fruit, badges, pens, pencils, erasers etc. As noted earlier in the book, all food needs to be provided within the provisions of Health and Safety regulations and the Food Safety Act 1990.

FIRST AID

An adequate first aid kit must be available and every leader should know where it is. Ideally all leaders will undergo some basic first aid training, but at least one person ought to train more fully with St

John's or the Red Cross and then keep their qualification up to date. In normal activities no drugs should ever be given, therefore none need be stored in the first aid box. For residential events minimal drugs like children's paracetemol or honey and glycerin pastilles for coughs may be needed, but if symptoms persist then a doctor should always be consulted.

When children register for activities it is important that you are made aware of any particular health problems (eg haemophilia), and that you have an emergency contact number or address in case of accident. For residential events a full health certificate should be required for every single child.

INSURANCE

Every children's activity needs to ensure that it has adequate insurance for public liability. Generally, to ensure against personal accident for everyone would be too expensive, though individual leaders may wish to cover themselves. Special care needs to be taken to make sure that churches' policies cover the children's work for all activities wherever they take place. Some policies refer to activities on the premises only, so home groups or outings are not covered. Wherever this is the case get the policy changed. Insurance cover for residential activities is essential.

If vehicles are being used for transporting children then every driver needs to ensure that they are properly insured, that all passengers wear seat belts (where provided), and that children behave appropriately whilst in the vehicle. Drivers should be seen to be suitable people for working with children, even if they are simply acting as transport and not regularly involved in the children's work.

If minibuses are being used, and *any* charge is being made, then they need to comply with the Transport Act 1985 in conjunction with the Minibus and Other Section 19 Permit Buses Regulations 1987 and the Minibus (Designated Bodies) Order 1987. (A full guide to this is available, entitled Passenger Transport Provided By Voluntary Groups PSV 385 July 1987.)

CONCLUSIONS

From this list of very practical considerations which fall into the lap of every leader or leadership team we see that there is a great deal involved in being a leader. Every aspect has at its heart a concern for the total well-being of the children and adults with whom we work. Christians should be operating at the highest level of standards and care. The leaders will often have to show everyone else the way. But, thankfully, they do not have to be perfect or able to do everything!

| ACTIVITIES |

1 Consider the following for your own involvement with children's work.
- Personal profiles
- Working agreements
- Training needs

2 Consider the practical considerations dealt with towards the end of the chapter, applying them to your own situation.

3 Make sure you act on your considerations of **1** and **2**.

| FURTHER READING |

Grow Your Own Leaders, Anton Baumohl, Scripture Union, 1987

Excellence In Leadership, John White, IVP, 1986

CHILDREN: THE BEST CHILDREN'S EVANGELISTS?

This book has been written for adults wanting to work with children, especially children from non-church backgrounds. Yet the people most in touch with children, apart from their parents, are other children. In playgroups and nurseries, in schools, out on the recreation grounds and even on the streets children get alongside each other. At times a gang can be very tightly knit, but by and large children are much more open to others joining in their games and activities than are adults. When it comes to running a holiday club, for example, all the publicity, school visits and brilliant advertising stunts are nothing compared to the pulling power of one child inviting another. So whatever you are planning, encourage children to invite their friends. Most of them will.

Children are also much more open to telling their friends about Jesus than adults seem to be. Perhaps because of an innocence or even naivety about how others might react, children will talk naturally about Jesus to their friends. We should certainly encourage them in this whilst helping them to be sensitive to their friends' different beliefs. In schools, children who have a real faith could also be encouraged to establish a school Bible club (see chapter 10). In these, as in all groups and clubs, children themselves should be encouraged to do as much of the planning and running as they are able to. This treats them as responsible people, respects their own thoughts and feelings and helps them develop their own gifts and talents. Responsible adults will need to be around to offer guidance and help whenever necessary, and occasionally to exercise any discipline that might be needed. In ways such as these children can act as witnesses to Jesus and some will even find that they are developing the gift of an evangelist. I have heard many stories of Christian children praying with their friends in the playground because their friend wanted to become part of God's family. When children from non-church families begin to follow Jesus they ought to be encouraged to share this with their parents. As suggested earlier there may well be times, perhaps every time, when it is best to suggest this is done by life rather than by word of mouth, with the child's changing lifestyle as evidence of the change Jesus has brought about. It is certainly important that our inward belief is outwardly expressed in word and deed (cf Romans 10:9), but I am not convinced that it is always best for the child's long term growth in discipleship to encourage them to speak out immediately to all and sundry.

All this having been said I want to express great caution about using children in direct evangelistic work. To allow them simply to witness naturally is right and good; to use them knocking on doors or in street evangelism is, for me, quite another thing. I have no problems about children joining in with their parents and the wider Christian family, for example, singing carols, marching for Jesus through the streets, being part of the all-age crowd (even being part of the all-age drama team) at street theatre or sketchboarding presentations. But to play on the vulnerability of children and use them as a softener in door to door work, or to get them to give out tracts because you know people will not react badly against them is for me very close to child abuse. The vulnerability of children is not a tool for our use. In my own experience, a number of sects have used children in this way. I can only confess to horror the first time I came across it in a mainstream Christian group. Where it is still happening I believe it should stop immediately. However excited the children involved can be, though they may actually be worried, scared or even bored, I believe this misuse of children is, in the long term, harmful to them.

When children were brought to Jesus they went back to their homes again to be cared for there. When Jesus himself at the age of twelve proved to be a gifted teacher and was able to astound the rabbis in the temple, he did not stay there, but instead returned to Nazareth to live in obedience to his parents. This was a better preparation for his life than making a name for himself as a child prodigy. Perhaps this was a temptation Jesus had to face at this early stage as much as those he faced later in the wilderness; power, popularity and success, or doing the Father's will?

Yes, children should be allowed, encouraged and helped to be witnesses for Jesus in their ordinary every day life. They should take part in all-age events which are evangelistic in nature, and be encouraged to invite their friends to events designed for them. But they should not be manipulated or used for evangelistic purposes. They are too precious to be damaged by such manipulation.

| ACTIVITIES |

Consider the issues discussed in
this brief chapter and work out any
implications for your own work.

A LIFETIME'S WORK

On a day retreat a church leadership team was asked to produce individual life maps on the role that the church had played in their lives from birth to the present. When sharing these in small groups one story went like this:

'During my childhood, church hardly featured; there were a few occasions that I remember though – a school service, a harvest event, and then there were the candlelight services at Christmas. But I don't remember anything more than that really. Then in my early twenties I met some Christians who made me begin to think about Christ. But it was not until I had my first baby that I really thought about it seriously; it was thinking about having him 'done' that actually brought me to commitment to Jesus.

But doing this exercise now has made me realise something for the first time; although few and far between, every childhood contact with the church was a good experience; I remember them all as very positive events; now I realise God was already working in my life then.'

As I heard the story it thrilled me, and reminded me again of a key part of the lifetime's work of children's evangelism. Very often children's workers will not see the real input of their work; it may be many, many years before the seed planted in childhood actually bursts forth into new life, but how thankful many are, and will be forever, that although they only really come to faith in the teenage or adult years, the seed was planted when they were children.

Reaching children should never be about rapid results: it is a lifetime's work. This should actually add to its importance and priority in the life of every local church because making Jesus known to children who have never heard the Good News, or only know the name of Jesus as a swear word or as the name of the baby born at Christmas, is an urgent task. The glory of God's name is at stake here. If we do not want to see God's name dragged through the mud in the coming generations then we need to share Jesus with children as well as adults. If the Decade of Evangelism is going to be of any lasting significance, then children's evangelism needs to be high on the agenda of every denomination and every local fellowship. Worldwide, if we are not involved in children's evangelism then we are ignoring billions of the world's population.

This task of making Jesus known is not simply a matter of telling children about Jesus; it is being concerned with every aspect of their welfare and working to end infant and child mortality – to promote the health, education, safety and overall well-being of every single child born on this planet. It is about longing for and working towards the end of child abuse in all its ugly forms. It is about taking children seriously. It is certainly not about being content with an attitude that rejoices if a child makes a real response to Jesus but ignores the hungry, the thirsty, the homeless, the unclaimed, the sick and imprisoned children of our world (cf Matthew 25:31–46). Nor should a child's family context be ignored or that child left without help for his or her ongoing spiritual development. Friendships need to be fostered, followers to be encouraged to keep on following even when the pathway seems to have disappeared, and members of a family need to deepen their relationships and discover the wider Christian family.

The long-term spiritual care of children should find its focus wherever and whenever possible in their homes, if we are to be true to the pattern of the scriptures, but the home will not be enough in itself. Children and their families will need the support and help of the larger family of faith which offers peer support to children, and to their parents or other carers. It will also offer an all-age setting for growth.

Parents and guardians should therefore be given help in sharing God within their home. This can be through prayer, Bible reading, activities, worship and, above all, seeking to live out the values and attitudes of God's rule in the home context. When this is not possible in a home where a child has developed their own faith then the wider church family must both seek to help the child's family and provide a context where the child can learn from experiencing these activities and joining in with others who also believe. As children they grow up and questions of faith arise then they should be encouraged to ask such questions. Doubt should be seen as a stepping stone for new growth rather than an expression of unbelief (especially perhaps in the teenage years). Every adult can help children to realise that they too are still growing and developing in their friendship with God.

How children are helped in the home will differ greatly from house to house depending on the particular lifestyle, gifts and make up of each household. There may be different patterns of prayer or different ways of reading the Bible; some households will make much of celebrating festivals together, others less so, and so on. Local fellowships should rejoice in diversity rather than try and squeeze everyone into the same mould.

There may well be a valuable role in setting up specific small groups for children to help them discover more about the faith together. Just as many churches have basics or nurture groups for adults they could run them for children as well. Personally I can see no reason why there could not be all-age basics groups as well. Careful planning would be required but they can work. As with everything else any such groups should be run with the parents' full awareness of all that takes place.

It has traditionally been of great importance that children are encouraged to pray and read the Bible for themselves, almost as soon as they are able to read. There are some excellent aids to help with this. Many children have found this personal discipline very valuable to them. But we need to ask whether this is always appropriate or the best method. If children learn better together through discovery then there must be limits to the value of purely personal Bible reading. This emphasises the importance of family or group discovery with members of the wider family of faith. Personally I feel that a blend of all these elements might be best, but each individual child will probably find one aspect more beneficial than others, and the particular aspect which is most beneficial at one stage of development may change with time as well.

The overall thrust of nurture will be a steadily growing faith; it is about long term care, a lifetime's work. Just as in creation human beings grow at different rates so they grow spiritually at different rates. There will be sudden bursts of growth and periods of apparent inaction. Different parts of our being develop at different rates too. In general our concern should be for all-round, balanced, healthy growth, to follow Jesus' great commandment, which is not to save souls but to make disciples, learners of Jesus. Children are the most avid learners of all. God is already at work in them, delighting to bring them into his kingdom without asking for anything other than that they receive it freely and openly. All we have to do is work with God and learn together with children how we should all live in God's kingdom.

THE CHILDREN ACT 1989

The Children Act 1989 is the most comprehensive piece of legislation regarding children ever enacted in the United Kingdom. Although passed in 1989 it only came into force in October 1991. The Act covers the following areas: parental responsibility; court proceedings; local authority services for children and families; children who are looked after by local authorities; the protection of children at risk; the welfare of children away from home; adoption, evidence, procedure and other matters.

The key concern of the whole Act is to support and encourage good practice in all work with children; and to ensure their safety. This central concern means that the Act should be warmly welcomed by all who care for the well-being of children. Large portions of the Act have no impact on the work that churches undertake with children, but that does not mean that it can or should be ignored; its concern for good practice should stimulate all of us afresh to evaluate the quality of our children's work.

Where the Act is most likely to impinge on church work is in their work with children under eight years old. Local authorities are now required to register all day care for children under eight which lasts for two or more hours in any one day.

All playgroups need to register with their local authority. Parent and toddler groups that last for more than two hours in a day need to register if any parent, or registered carer, is not present with the child throughout the session.

Children's holidays involving under eights would need to register.

Creches provided for shoppers need to be registered if they last for more than two hours in a day.

Many activities will not need to register because they last for less than two hours. Sunday groups, midweek clubs etc will usually fall into this category. But if they last for more than two hours and include children under eight without their parents constantly present then registration will be required.

If an event occurs less than six times a year it will normally be exempt. Hence a holiday club may not require registration because it may only last for five days. If you were to run two in a year, however, or a longer club you should register with your local authority.

All activities required to register will be inspected. Particular concern will be taken over who is working with or has access to children and over the suitability of the premises. The particular factors on suitability of people were detailed in chapter 14 of the book.

All of the above is only a very brief introduction and outline of the Act. The reality is that as local authorities have to interpret and implement the Act there are inevitably differences of practice from one authority to another. If in any doubt, contact should be made with the local social services department. If you have any doubts about whether or not you need to register do not take the risk of running an activity for under eights without consulting the local authority first.

Further Information

A particularly helpful brief guide is available from the Children's Work Team of the Methodist Division for Education and Youth, 2 Chester House, Pages Lane, Muswell Hill, London N10 1PR.

HMSO publish a series of guides to the Children Act. The one relevant to Voluntary organisations is the blue guide.

Contact your own local authority for their own guidelines; they all have them.

For information on legislation in Australia and New Zealand contact Scripture Union at the Australian National Office, 241 Flinders Lane, Melbourne 3000 or the New Zealand National Office, PO Box 760, Wellington.